CAPITALISM

ABOUT THE AUTHOR

GARRY LEECH is the author of numerous books, including *The FARC: The Longest Insurgency* (Zed Books, 2011); *The Failure of Global Capitalism: From Cape Breton to Colombia and Beyond* (CBU Press, 2009); *Beyond Bogotá: Diary of a Drug War Journalist in Colombia* (Beacon Press, 2009); and *Crude Interventions: The United States, Oil and the New World (Dis)order* (Zed Books, 2006). He is director of the Centre for International Studies and a lecturer in the Department of Political Science at Cape Breton University, Canada.

OTHER BOOKS BY GARRY LEECH
AVAILABLE FROM ZED BOOKS

Crude Interventions: The United States, Oil and the New World (Dis)order
The FARC: The Longest Insurgency

CAPITALISM

A Structural Genocide

GARRY LEECH

ZED BOOKS
London & New York

para Johan, Miguel y Kathleen, con todo mi amor

Capitalism: A Structural Genocide was first published in 2012
by Zed Books Ltd, 7 Cynthia Street, London N1 9JF, UK
and Room 400, 175 Fifth Avenue, New York, NY 10010, USA

www.zedbooks.co.uk

Designed and typeset in ITC Bodoni Twelve
by illuminati, Grosmont
Index by John Barker
Cover designed by Rogue Four Design
Printed and bound in Great Britain
by CPI Group (UK) Ltd, Croydon CRO 4YY

FSC
www.fsc.org
MIX
Paper from
responsible sources
FSC® C013604

Distributed in the USA exclusively by Palgrave Macmillan, a division
of St Martin's Press, LLC, 175 Fifth Avenue, New York, NY 10010, USA

A catalogue record for this book is available from the British Library
Library of Congress Cataloging in Publication Data available

ISBN 978 1 78032 200 1 hb
ISBN 978 1 78032 199 8 pb

CONTENTS

ACKNOWLEDGEMENTS

This book would not have been possible without the valuable intellectual insights provided to me by many people over the years or without the diverse array of exhilarating experiences that have enriched my life. With regard to the more immediate task of actually putting my thoughts down on paper for this book, I owe a huge debt of gratitude to Jim Sacouman and James J. Brittain for their profound insights and inspiration. I would also like to thank Barb Moore, Zelda Abramson, Heather A. Kitchin and Karen J. Turner for the various ways in which they contributed to this project. I am also grateful to Steve Law for his insightful reading of the manuscript and valuable feedback, and to my editors Ken Barlow, Robin Gable and Lucy Morton for their invaluable contribution to this project. I am deeply indebted to my wife Terry for her unwavering support during the writing of this book and of my work in general. Finally, I have written this book in an effort to illustrate that we can indeed create a better world, not just for the sake of my children Johan, Owen and Morgan, and my granddaughter Kathleen, but for the sake of future generations everywhere.

INTRODUCTION

Philosophers have hitherto only interpreted the world in various
ways; the point is to change it.

Karl Marx

Over the past thirty years, I have travelled and worked extensively in Latin America. During this time I could not help
but notice that significant portions of the population of Latin
America endure degrees of poverty inconceivable to most people
in North America – the United States and Canada. Furthermore,
in many places, the degree of poverty has not diminished over
these decades, and inequality has actually increased. These
observations from my time in Latin America led me to question
why such disparities exist between the majority of the population
in North America, who are relatively wealthy, and the majority of
people in Latin America, who continue to endure such hardship.
After all, this disparity exists in a hemisphere – indeed, in a
world – that contains more than a sufficient supply of resources
to ensure that everyone's basic needs are met.[1]

One of the most profound and depressing experiences I had
in Latin America occurred when I was travelling alone in a
canoe down the Napo river in the Ecuadorian Amazon in 1989.

I spent almost two weeks on the Napo and stayed with several indigenous families. The most prominent indigenous groups in the Napo region are the Huaorani, Cofan, Secoya and Quichua, all of whom had succeeded in remaining isolated from the outside world until the middle of the twentieth century. By the time I visited the region, many of those indigenous families living along the banks of the Napo had become accustomed to outsiders. But other clans still lived relatively isolated deeper in the rainforest. The indigenous people living along the Napo had retained much of their traditional way of life, but one of the families that I stayed with was markedly different than the others. That particular family consisted of a father and his 5-year-old daughter, and they had a melancholy and a defeated air that was truly disturbing.

Most of the wood and thatched houses in the village had been abandoned and only a handful of inhabitants remained. I learned that an oil company had arrived in the village sixteen years earlier. The company promised the indigenous inhabitants jobs and a better life. So they abandoned their traditional lifestyle, which consisted of hunting, fishing and gathering forest crops. They no longer had to engage in these practices because the company provided them with all the food and goods they needed in return for their labour. The indigenous villagers came to believe that life would always be that way. But the oil ran out one year before I arrived in the village and it was difficult for the indigenous to return to their traditional ways of life because the oil had polluted the forest and streams. Also, many of the younger indigenous people had little interest in learning the traditional ways – of which they knew very little – after experiencing the 'modern' life that the company had provided through the provision of such amenities as alcohol, Coca-Cola, canned food, electricity and many other things. Ultimately, finding it difficult to sustain themselves in the aftermath of the company's departure, many of the people, including the mother of the 5-year-old girl I met, abandoned the village and went in search of jobs in Ecuador's cities in a desperate and often futile attempt to recapture the 'modern' world. The indigenous inhabitants of that

Insomnia

remote village, those who remained and those who had left, were stuck between two worlds: the traditional world they could not return to because of the ecological destruction wrought by the oil company and the 'modern' world and its promises of wealth and material riches that were beyond their grasp.

Tragically, I would later learn that the story of this small indigenous village was not unique. US-based multinational oil companies, including Texaco, Occidental, Conoco, Amoco, ARCO, Unocal and Mobil, had been operating throughout the Napo region of the Amazon since the 1960s with devastating consequences for the indigenous population and the rainforest. The operations of oil companies dumped untreated chemicals and industrial solvents into the waters of the rainforest. Texaco alone spilled 16.8 million gallons of oil into the Ecuadorian Amazon – more than one-and-a-half times as much as spilled in the *Exxon Valdez* disaster in Alaska.[2] As a result, the rates of cancer, miscarriage and birth defects in the region are now significantly higher than in the rest of Ecuador, with hundreds of deaths having resulted from the oil operations that extracted the valuable resource, not for the benefit of the local population, but to ensure the continuance of the materialistically comfortable lifestyles of North America.[3]

And so, almost five hundred years after the arrival of the Spanish conquistadors, the indigenous in the Ecuadorian Amazon had become victims of yet another conquest. This time, instead of Spaniards wielding swords and cannons, the new conquistadors were US corporations that had come armed with oil drilling equipment and promises of a better life. The repercussions of that conquest were what I witnessed in that desolate village. It was difficult to grasp the devastation that had been visited on that small indigenous community and its culture, first by the arrival of the oil company and then by its departure.

This and other experiences in Latin America led to me delve into the causes of such widespread human suffering. Ultimately, the conclusion I reached was that the structures of global capitalism, while providing impressive opportunities for wealth generation, also ensure that the wealth generated remains in the hands of a small minority. I also came to realize that these structures contribute to the deaths of millions of people around the world annually. Are these deaths simply unavoidable casualties on the inevitable march of progress? Or do they constitute a form of genocide?

There are many examples throughout history of direct physical violence on a massive scale being utilized on behalf of capital – the annihilation of indigenous people in the Americas, the slave trade, World War I, and so on – but these can easily be dismissed as exceptions to the norm given the relatively sporadic nature of their occurrence. Therefore, to effectively argue that capitalism constitutes genocide it is crucial to show that violence is inherent in the internal logic of capital and, therefore, that it is a permanent feature of the capitalist system. I will argue that both of these factors are in fact true, and that the form that the violence takes is structural. Furthermore, not only is this structural violence inherent in the capitalist system, but it results in death on a genocidal scale, thereby constituting a class-based structural genocide that targets the poor, particularly in the global South.

In order to make the case that capitalism constitutes structural genocide, it is first necessary to examine the concept of structural violence. According to Johan Galtung, social injustice and inequality, both in power and in wealth, lie at the core of structural violence when they result from social structures that disproportionately benefit one group of people while preventing others from meeting their fundamental needs. Therefore *social structures* that cause human suffering and death constitute structural violence.

Utilizing various definitions of genocide, it is possible to expand the concept of structural violence in order to define structural genocide. To achieve this I will draw on various theories of genocide as well as on the United Nations' Genocide Convention and the Rome Statute of the International Criminal Court to demonstrate why the structural violence inherent in capitalism constitutes structural genocide. Ultimately, it is not my intention to argue simply that the capitalist system – or even those managing the system – be held accountable in a court of law. Rather, I will use the various definitions of genocide to highlight the illegitimacy of a social system in which structural violence on a massive scale constitutes an inherent component. The point is not to engage in polemics, but to argue that there are solid analytical and political reasons to use the term 'genocide'.

In order to determine whether capitalism constitutes structural genocide, it is necessary first to establish that structural violence is inherent in the capitalist system – since the latter is a prerequisite for the former. This will be achieved through an examination of the internal logic of capital by engaging in a critique of the market economy and liberal democracy; the commodification of labour power and land, and by extension people and nature; the inherently expansive and exploitative nature of capital in its drive for profit; the dispossession of increasing numbers of people from their land and livelihoods; and the ecological crisis that results.

Capital's internal logic forces it to expand to every corner of the globe, and the resulting inequality and deprivation of basic needs for billions of people are inherent components of capitalism. These inequalities in wealth and power constitute a form of structural violence that targets large sectors of the world's population, particularly people living in the global South, because it necessarily deprives them of their fundamental needs.

Four case studies will be examined in order to illustrate how capitalism constitutes structural genocide perpetrated against tens of millions of people in the twenty-first century. The first case study shows how so-called free-market policies implemented under the North American Free Trade Agreement (NAFTA) have forcibly dispossessed almost 2 million Mexican farmers of their lands and livelihoods. The failure of Mexican farmers to compete with cheaper, subsidized agricultural imports from the United States has resulted in a flood of dispossessed peasants to urban areas in a desperate and often fruitless search for jobs. The structural violence that dispossessed farmers and others of their livelihoods has also resulted in many becoming victims of the physical violence that has flourished in the midst of the related social breakdown and that has killed tens of thousands of people in recent years. This violence has most visibly manifested itself in the form of turf wars between competing drug cartels and the Mexican army and in the femicide occurring in cities situated along the border with the United States. Many dispossessed farmers and other impoverished Mexicans have become economic refugees, with thousands dying in their desperate attempts to cross illegally the border with the United States in search of a viable means of subsistence.

The second case study examines farmer suicides in India. Under neoliberal globalization, hundreds of thousands of farmers in India began borrowing money in order to purchase genetically modified (GM) and hybrid seeds patented under the WTO's intellectual property rights regime. These seeds were supposed to increase their yields and, by extension, their incomes, but when the promised increases in yields failed to materialize Indian farmers were unable to pay off their debts. In many cases, these farmers had to borrow more money in order to purchase new seeds in a desperate struggle to pay off previous loans. The inability of Mexican farmers to compete with cheap imports from the United States eventually made them increasingly vulnerable to physical violence at the hands of others; the same structural violence has resulted in many Indian farmers also dying from physical violence – but often at their own hands. Since 1997, more than 200,000 Indian farmers have committed suicide – seeing no other honourable means of escaping the spiralling debts that resulted from their integration into the global capitalist system.[4]

The third case study illustrates how structural violence not only makes people increasingly vulnerable to direct physical violence – either at the hands of others or at their own hands – but actually kills people directly. More than 10 million people globally die each year from hunger and from preventable and treatable diseases such as malaria, diarrhoea, tuberculosis and

AIDS, with sub-Saharan Africa the region most seriously impacted.[5] This structural genocide is a direct consequence of acts that adhere to the logic of capital, which ensures food security for the global North and significant profits for agribusinesses and pharmaceuticals companies, but fails to see value in human beings whose labour power is not required and who are too poor to be consumers.

The fourth and final case study examines how capitalism is unsustainable from an ecological perspective, and argues that this constitutes a form of structural genocide against future generations. The logic of capital requires constant growth in order to accumulate wealth, but this growth is dependent on the destruction of nature. Inevitably, the drive to maximize profits that lies at the root of the logic of capital requires that essential natural resources be exploited in an unsustainable manner – to benefit disproportionately a wealthy minority at the expense of the basic needs of the majority. This process not only constitutes structural genocide perpetrated by the haves against the have-nots today, it also represents structural genocide against future generations who will not be able to meet their basic needs.

I have chosen these particular case studies for two reasons. First, they illustrate that the massive human suffering that occurs under capitalism is not limited to a specific geographic region – it exists on every continent and will also impact future generations. And, second, each case study illustrates a particular form of the mass human suffering and violence that result from the structures of capitalism. As these case studies make evident, social injustice and inequality are inherent in capitalism, and the resulting structural violence constitutes a catastrophe of genocidal proportions. Therefore capitalism constitutes a class-based structural genocide that targets the poor and should not be viewed as a legitimate system under which to organize society. And yet capitalism is viewed as just this by hundreds of millions of people around the world. Therefore it is important to examine the hegemonic processes that ensure a social system that is genocidal manages not only to perpetuate itself, but also to be celebrated. The hegemonic discourse of capital is perpetuated through the media, education and culture in order to preserve the dominant paradigm. Capitalist philanthropy will also be examined, since it serves the interests of capital by helping to generate consent for the system among many peoples, particularly in the global South.

But it is not enough to conclude that capitalism constitutes structural genocide and therefore should be viewed as an illegitimate social system; it is crucial that we also look at what a radical social transformation to a more democratic, egalitarian and sustainable alternative might look like. I conclude by examining some basic principles that could provide a foundation upon which to build real socialist alternatives that emphasize human development and ecological sustainability. With these principles in mind, I briefly reflect on the emergence of socialist experiments in contemporary Latin America, particularly the cases of Venezuela and Cuba. Finally, I examine the necessity of incorporating 'ecosocialist' approaches into any socialist models in order to address the ecological crisis effectively. Ultimately, a revolutionary transformation is essential if we are to bring an end to capitalism's structural genocide.

In conclusion, this book focuses on capitalism as structural genocide and argues that a more humane alternative social system could end this catastrophe. It does not, however, claim that all structural violence and structural genocide are a consequence of capitalism. For instance, female circumcision and infanticide are largely culturally driven, and a new social system would still have to contend with these forms of structural violence and structural genocide. The core argument made in this book is that capitalism constitutes structural genocide; and while structural genocide can also occur under socialism, it is not inherent in that social system. Ultimately, I will make evident that the catastrophe I witnessed in that remote indigenous village in the Ecuadorian Amazon is being visited in one form or another on billions of people throughout the global South by a genocidal capitalist system.

I

WHAT IS STRUCTURAL GENOCIDE?

> Any fool can build an economic system where rich people buy expensive products.
>
> *Johan Galtung*

Each year millions of people throughout the world die of hunger, perish in childbirth and succumb to AIDS and other preventable and treatable diseases. Are these tragedies acts of God, perpetrated for some reason beyond the comprehension of human beings? Are they simply the result of the whims of nature? Or, as previously mentioned, are they unfortunate tragedies of the inevitable march of progress? We in the global North are repeatedly bombarded with solicitations from organizations such as CARE, Oxfam and World Vision for donations to aid the seemingly never-ending plight of hungry, sick and homeless people in the global South. We are told that they are less fortunate than we; and therefore that we have an obligation to help. But we are rarely told the cause of their suffering, beyond the 'random' acts of nature such as drought or hurricanes that devastate these people's lives. The implication is that such massive human suffering is tragic, but that there is no specific guilty party. And if someone is to blame, then it is usually the victims themselves. After all, isn't their suffering largely a result of their failure to achieve the same level of 'development' as that enjoyed by most people in the global North? If only we could help them to develop, to modernize, then surely much of this human suffering could be averted. But is this true? Or is the tragic suffering endured by people in the global South directly linked to our relatively comfortable material existence in the global North? More importantly, are this mass misery and death caused by acts of violence resulting from human actions? But how could this be when there is no evidence of any direct physical aggression being perpetrated against the victims? According to Johan Galtung, many of these people are indeed victims of violence; and that violence is structural.

Galtung argues that violence is 'the avoidable impairment of fundamental human needs or, to put it in more general terms, the impairment of human life, which lowers the actual degree to which someone is able to meet their needs below that which would otherwise be possible'.[1] Thus, he expands the definition of violence beyond acts of direct physical violence to include also human suffering caused by social structures that disproportionately benefit some people while diminishing the ability of others to meet their fundamental needs. As such, argues David Roberts, 'Violence ... could be committed directly and deliberately, but could also be conducted indirectly and largely unintentionally, by structures populated by humans.'[2] Similarly, anthropologist Paul Farmer suggests, 'Structural violence is violence exerted systematically – that is, indirectly – by everyone who belongs to a certain social order ... In short, the concept of structural violence is intended to inform the study of the social machinery of oppression'.[3]

According to Galtung, social injustice lies at the heart of structural violence because it manifests itself in inequality – in the distribution of both wealth and power. As such, notes Galtung, structural violence is marked by

> *the difference between the potential and the actual*, between what could have been and what is. ... Thus, if a person died of tuberculosis in the eighteenth century it would be hard to conceive of this as

violence since it might have been quite unavoidable, but if he dies from it today, despite all the medical resources in the world, then violence is present according to our definition.[4]

In other words, in contemporary times, deaths from tuberculosis are not a consequence of insufficient medical knowledge, but rather they result from a lack of access to that medical knowledge due to social structures. Therefore, as anthropologist Paul Farmer explains, 'Structural violence is visited upon all those whose social status denies them access to the fruits of scientific and social progress.'[5]

Structural violence manifests itself in many ways, but its common theme is the deprivation of people's basic needs as a result of the existing social structures. Those basic needs include food, health care and other resources essential for achieving a healthy existence and the fullest human development possible. Such inequality is rooted in the oppression of one group by another. And, as Paulo Freire argues, those structures that result in oppression constitute structural violence:

> Any situation in which 'A' objectively exploits 'B' and hinders his and her pursuit of self-affirmation as a responsible person is one of oppression. Such a situation in itself constitutes violence, even when sweetened by false generosity, because it interferes with the individual's ontological and historical vocation to be more fully human. With the establishment of a relationship of oppression, violence has *already* begun.[6]

Even though structural violence affects millions of people around the world, it is not as visible a form of violence as direct physical violence. In fact, it often appears anonymous to the degree that people are not even aware that there is a perpetrator. Galtung addresses the insidious nature of structural violence:

> There may not be any person who directly harms another person in the structure. The violence is built into the structure and shows up as unequal power and consequently as unequal life chances. *Resources* are unevenly distributed ... Above all the *power to decide over the distribution of resources* is unevenly distributed.[7]

Ultimately, if a social system creates and maintains inequality in both power and wealth that benefits certain social groups while preventing others from meeting their fundamental needs, even if unintentionally, then structural violence exists. And if such inequality is inherent in a social system, then so is structural violence.

DEFINING STRUCTURAL GENOCIDE

Structural violence does not always result in death. But when structural violence results in death on a mass scale, does it constitute structural genocide? In order to answer this question we must first define structural genocide. Numerous instances of what has commonly been labelled as 'genocide' have been perpetrated from the earliest days of the capitalist era, beginning with the annihilation of the indigenous peoples of the Americas in order to access the natural resources that were used to fuel Europe's Industrial Revolution. However, genocide was not legally defined until 1948 when the United Nations Convention on the Prevention and Punishment of the Crime of Genocide (CPPCG) was approved by the UN General Assembly.

Article II of the CPPCG, which came into force in 1951, defines genocide as

> any of the following acts committed with intent to destroy, in whole or in part, a national, ethnical, racial or religious, group, as such: (a) killing members of the group; (b) causing serious bodily or mental harm to members of the group; (c) deliberately inflicting on the group conditions of life calculated to bring about its physical destruction in whole or in part; (d) imposing measures intended to prevent births within the group; (e) forcibly transferring children of the group to another group.[8]

The definition of genocide according to the CPPCG recognizes national, ethnic, racial and religious groups as victims but not political groups. As such, mass deaths of people based on their political views and social class would not constitute an act of genocide according to the CPPCG. The absence of political groups is surprising given that the CPPCG was a response to the Holocaust in which the Nazis targeted not only racial and religious groups, but also political groups, particularly socialists and communists.[9]

The first session of the UN General Assembly in 1946 had already adopted a resolution condemning genocide that included political groups among its definition of victims. And the following year, when the first draft of the Genocide Convention was formulated, it also included violence perpetrated against political groups and suggested that death on a massive scale that results from structural violence could be considered genocide. This draft included in its definition of genocide any act

> Causing the death of members of a group or injuring their health or physical integrity by ... (b) subjection to conditions of life which, by lack of proper housing, clothing, food, hygiene and medical care, or excessive work or physical exertion are likely to result in the debilitation or death of the individuals; or ... (d) deprivation of all means of livelihood, by confiscation of property, looting, curtailment of work, denial of housing and of supplies otherwise available to the other inhabitants of the territory concerned.[10]

In addition to noting that political groups had been targeted in the Holocaust, some delegates involved in drawing up the Convention also pointed out that, in the Cold War context, ideology had become a core issue in internal and international conflicts and that, as a result, some political groups were in as much, if not more, danger than other groups.[11] Nevertheless, the term 'political groups' was removed from the text of the final draft of the Convention at the eleventh hour after much debate, due to pressure from national leaders concerned that their violent suppression of domestic political opposition might make them vulnerable to charges of genocide. The Soviet Union was first and foremost among this group due to Stalin's concern that his purges might be classified as an act of genocide.[12] As international law scholar Beth van Schaack notes, the exclusion of political groups from the CPPCG 'resulted in a legal regime that insulates political leaders from being charged with the very crime that they may be most likely to commit: the extermination of politically threatening groups'.[13]

Similarly, Ervin Staub argues in his book *The Roots of Evil: The Origins of Genocide and Other Group Violence*,

> Killing groups of people for political reasons has become the primary form of genocide (and mass killing) in our time. ... [Therefore] genocide means an attempt to exterminate a racial, ethnic, religious, cultural, or political group, either directly through murder or indirectly by creating conditions that lead to the group's destruction.[14]

Staub refers to Cambodia under Pol Pot (1975–79) as an example of a politically motivated genocide, and to Argentina under its military junta (1976–83) as a politically motivated mass killing, with the difference between the two being the numbers of people killed – as many as 2 million in Cambodia and approximately 30,000 in Argentina.[15] Not only does Staub include political groups in his definition, but his reference to any attempt to exterminate '*indirectly* by creating conditions that lead to the group's destruction' clearly suggests that structural violence could constitute a means. Ultimately, Schaack argues,

> Discarding political groups from the Genocide Convention created an internally inconsistent human rights regime, because other major international agreements include this category. The prohibition of crimes against humanity prohibits persecutions on 'political, racial or religious grounds.' Likewise, the provisions of the Refugee Convention protect individuals from persecution on account of 'race, religion, nationality, membership in a particular social group, or political opinion.' These longstanding instruments reflect the guiding international legal prohibition on the extermination or persecution of individuals on the basis of their political affiliations or opinions. ... The loophole created by the [Genocide Convention] drafting committee's exclusion of political groups does not hold up in this context.[16]

The same motivations that prevented the category of 'political groups' from being included in the CPPCG when it was approved by the General Assembly in 1948 have also blocked all subsequent attempts to revise the Convention to include it. Governments continue to remain wary of being accused of genocide for perpetrating politically or ideologically motivated acts of violence. In 1998, at the Rome Conference, which established the International Criminal Court (ICC), Cuba was the only country to argue for an amendment to the Genocide Convention to include political and social groups – a proposal that was promptly quashed. However, the definition of 'crimes against humanity' was expanded at the conference to include crimes perpetrated during times of peace in addition to those committed in war.[17]

While genocide has commonly been called the 'crime of crimes', the ICC has deemed genocide, crimes against humanity and war crimes to be of equal gravity.[18] The Rome Statute gives jurisdiction to the ICC over the 'most serious crimes of concern to the international community as a whole', which it defines as genocide, crimes against humanity, war crimes and aggression.[19] Interestingly, and seemingly contradictorily, the Rome Statute includes 'genocide' not only as a separate crime, but also as a crime against humanity through the inclusion of the act of 'extermination' in its list of 'crimes against humanity'. The Rome Statute defines the act of extermination as 'the intentional infliction of conditions of life, *inter alia* the deprivation of access to food and medicine, calculated to bring about the destruction of part of a population'.[20] This definition of extermination is virtually identical to Article 2(c) of the Genocide Convention, which defines genocide as any act 'deliberately inflicting on the group conditions of life calculated to bring about its physical destruction in whole or in part'. However, unlike the definition of genocide, the definition of crimes against humanity includes the persecution of any identifiable group or collectivity on political grounds.

Both of these definitions contain wording that relates to two of the most crucial components in a definition of structural genocide: structural violence as a means and intentionality as a motivating factor. Neither of these definitions specifies that genocide must result from direct physical violence, and the words 'inflicting on the group conditions of life calculated to bring about its physical destruction in whole or in part' suggests that structural violence could be considered a means for perpetrating genocide. In fact, as Hannibal Travis has pointed out, 'It is becoming widely recognized by scholars that famines for which a state bears responsibility are justly classified as a form of genocide.'[21] But those scholars, including Travis, who address the concept of structural genocide, tend to focus on the state as the culprit rather than holding the internal logic of a social system responsible. Nevertheless, the concept of structural genocide has gained significant legitimacy among scholars and experts on international law.

The definition of 'genocide' in the Genocide Convention and that of 'extermination' as a crime against humanity both clearly state that a genocidal act must be 'deliberate' or 'intentional'. But since we are defining structural genocide, the issue here is not so much the 'intent' of individuals, but rather the 'intent' of the structures of a social system. The 'intentional' outcomes of actions that adhere to a particular social system are directly determined by the logic of that system. Therefore, if adhering to the logic of a social system inevitably results in structural violence that causes death on a mass scale, then it is apparent that structural genocide is an intentional outcome of human behaviours that adhere to that logic. Furthermore, as historian Ben Kiernan argues in reference to deaths resulting from state policies in the Sudan,

> If those perpetrators did not set out to commit genocide, it was a predictable result of their actions.... When such policies, purposefully pursued, knowingly bring genocidal results, their perpetrators may be legally judged to have possessed the 'intent' to destroy a group, at least 'in part', whatever their motive.[22]

The legal norm that Kiernan is referring to, which is relevant to both intentionality and the definition of structural genocide, is the doctrine of wilful blindness. In May 2011, US Supreme Court Justice Samuel Alito stated:

> The doctrine of willful blindness is well established in criminal law ... and courts applying the doctrine of willful blindness hold that defendants cannot escape the reach of these statutes by deliberately shielding themselves from clear evidence of critical facts that are strongly suggested by the circumstances.[23]

In other words, if actions adhering to the logic of a social system knowingly result in outcomes (i.e. structural genocide) other than those intended, those outcomes cannot simply be dismissed as unintentional due to the wilful blindness of those carrying out those actions.

The Extraordinary Chambers in the Courts of Cambodia, established under an agreement between the United Nations and the Cambodian government as a tribunal for investigating and prosecuting crimes perpetrated by the Khymer Rouge between 1975 and 1979, similarly defined 'intentionality' with regard to crimes against humanity and viewed structural violence as a means. In the trial of Guek Eav Kaing, the commander of the S21 detention centre, the Court stated:

> In many instances prisoners were deliberately killed through a variety of means. In other instances the perpetrators may not have intended to kill, but were aware that death could occur as a result of their conduct, for example when they beat or tortured prisoners. ... The living conditions imposed at S21 were calculated to bring about the deaths of detainees. These conditions included but were not limited to the deprival of access to adequate food and medical care. ... The unlawful deaths of over 12,380 detainees which occurred as a result of murder or the imposition of living conditions calculated to bring about death, constituted the mass killing of members of a civilian population.[24]

Thus the Court stated that structural violence through the imposition of living conditions, such as a lack of access to adequate food and medical care, constituted a means through which to kill people, while actions, such as beatings and torture, likely to result in death constituted 'intent'. Furthermore, with regard to political motivation, the Court noted, 'Detainees were denied these fundamental rights based upon their real or perceived political beliefs or political opposition to those in power'.[25] In 2010, the Court convicted Kaing of persecution on political grounds that constituted crimes against humanity, including extermination.

So while Kiernan holds the state responsible for the genocide in the Sudan, and the Khymer Rouge tribunal convicted a state official for extermination in Cambodia, the definitions of intentionality in both cases – as well as the inclusion of political motivation in the Cambodian example – are relevant to cases of structural genocide that result from actions carried out in adherence to the logic of a social system – where deaths result not solely from direct physical violence, but also from ideologically motivated acts that knowingly deprive people of their basic needs.

Political scientist Nafeez Mosaddeq Ahmed is one of the few scholars to examine structural genocide occurring under different social systems. Ahmed analyses the social structures of communist collectivization and capitalist imperialism, including in the era of neoliberal globalization. He argues that conventional definitions of genocide should be broadened to include mass deaths resulting from transnational structural violence:

> This form of structural violence, through the international economic order's systematic generation of human insecurity, has led to the deaths of countless hundreds of millions of people, and the deprivation of thousands of millions of others. Most of the literature on human security, development, and genocide fails to see this phenomenon of global mass death and marginalization – a consequence of structurally-induced deprivation – as a form of genocide.[26]

CONCLUSION

As we have seen, there are legitimate arguments suggesting that genocide perpetrated against any group or collectivity on political grounds can result from structural violence and that it is 'intentional' when an act 'knowingly' results in death on a mass scale. Therefore structural genocide can be defined as structural violence that intentionally inflicts on any group or collectivity conditions of life that bring about its physical destruction in whole or in part.

Defining structural genocide is one issue, while responding to a systemic crisis of such magnitude is another matter entirely. International law focuses on the actions of individuals and is not capable of addressing systemic crimes. As previously noted with regard to structural violence, it is difficult to point the finger at one or even a handful of individuals precisely because the violence is structural. And, as Joel Kovel notes in reference to the capitalist system, it is

> structural because the behavior of elites cannot be reduced to ordinary motivations like greed or domination, as greedy or domineering as they may in fact be. When we are talking of class interest and of how individuals become personifications of great institutional forces, all the innumerable variations that make the human psyche interesting are subjected to a few basic rules, and a remarkable uniformity of behavior prevails.[27]

Therefore structural genocide in a capitalist system would be perpetrated by the 'remarkable uniformity of behaviour' of one class (capitalists, with the complicity of consumers largely in the global North) against another class (workers, broadly defined to include peasants and those surviving in the informal sector, particularly in the global South).[28] In short, it would constitute a class-based structural genocide or what sociologist Michael Mann has called 'classicide', which refers to 'the intended mass killing of entire social classes'.[29] Mann applies the term 'classicide' to the atrocities perpetrated by communist regimes such as that headed by Pol Pot in Cambodia, in which the intellectual – in essence, the old ruling – class was targeted primarily through direct physical violence. But the structural violence inherent in capitalism referred to by Mosaddeq Ahmed could just as easily be construed as a form of classicide perpetrated by the capitalist class against the working classes, particularly in the global South.

Ultimately, if a sufficient number of deaths occur globally as a result of conscious actions adhering to the logic of capital, it could be argued that the structural violence in capitalism constitutes structural genocide. And, regardless of which specific individuals constitute the capitalist class, structural genocide would persist because they are compelled to abide by the internal logic of capital. Therefore it is the capitalist system that is guilty of structural genocide.

Clearly, it is not feasible to advocate bringing an entire social system to justice in a courtroom or before an ad hoc tribunal.[30] Therefore the objective here is to use legal and theoretical definitions of genocide as a means by which to question the legitimacy of the capitalist system and the desirability of organizing a society according to such an ideology.

By utilizing the concept of structural violence as characterized by Galtung and others it has been possible to establish a definition of structural genocide. The question that remains is whether or not capitalism constitutes structural genocide. In order to determine this, an examination of the internal logic of capital is required.

2

THE LOGIC OF CAPITAL

Marx has never been so useful and necessary in order to understand and transform the world, today even more so than yesterday.

Samir Amin

Before we can determine whether or not capitalism constitutes structural genocide, we must first establish that structural violence is an inherent component of the capitalist system. In order to do this, we need to examine the internal logic of capital and the way in which it determines how the capitalist system functions.

In theory, capitalism is a social system organized around a free-market economy and private property. According to economist Ludwig von Mises,

The market economy is the social system of the division of labour under private ownership of the means of production ... The market is a process, actuated by the interplay of the actions of the various individuals cooperating under the division of labor. The forces determining the – continually changing – state of the market are the value judgments of these individuals and their actions as directed by these value judgments. ... There is nothing inhuman or mystical with regard to the market. The market process is entirely a resultant of human actions. Every market phenomenon can be traced back to definite choices of the members of the market society.[1]

As Mises makes clear, there is nothing natural about the 'market'; it is 'entirely a resultant of human actions' – those of producers and consumers. Furthermore, Karl Polanyi argues that the market's role as the dominant central component of the capitalist system is unique in the economic history of human-kind: 'While history and ethnography know of various kinds of economies, most of them comprising the institution of markets, they know of no economy prior to our own, even approximately controlled and regulated by markets.'[2]

The principal feature in this market system is another human construct: capital. And capital constitutes the engine that drives the capitalist system. Capital can come in many forms (i.e. money, land, buildings, machinery, goods produced, etc.) and its purpose is self-expansion through the generation of profit and rents, which constitutes capital accumulation. Consequently, as Mises explained, 'The notion of capital makes sense only in the market economy. It serves the deliberations and calculations of individuals or groups of individuals operating on their own account in such an economy. It is a device of capitalists, entrepreneurs and farmers eager to make profits and to avoid losses.'[3] In essence, capitalists use their money as capital to generate profits, which translate into more capital, thereby achieving capital accumulation. As Karl Marx noted, 'The economic character of *capitalist* becomes firmly fixed to a man only if his money constantly functions as *capital*.'[4] Consequently, as Joel Kovel explains, 'When we say "capital does this" or that, we mean that certain human actions are carried out according to the logic of capital.'[5]

The capitalist uses capital to generate more capital by producing a commodity that has a 'use-value' (i.e. satisfies a social need) and then selling it on the market where the capitalist receives its 'exchange-value', which is determined in theory by supply and demand, but often in reality by speculative trading and monopolistic practices. The money that the capitalist pockets after covering the costs of production, including labour costs, represents the 'surplus value', which translates into profit. Obviously a variety of factors influence the cost of production, but, basically, if labour costs increase and the exchange-value of the commodity produced remains constant, then workers gain a greater percentage of the surplus value. Conversely, if labour costs are reduced and exchange value remains constant then the capitalist increases his or her share of surplus value.

The profits generated constitute an accumulation of capital that the capitalist can then reinvest to produce more commodities in order to generate more profits. Thus capitalism constantly expands, and, as sociologist John Bellamy Foster notes, 'The driving force of this expansion is capital accumulation and the search for ever expanding profits.'[6] Logically, then, in a capitalist system, nothing has value until it is brought to market and its exchange-value is realized. In other words, nature in its natural state is worthless according to the logic of capital; it only achieves value – either 'use-value' or 'exchange-value' – once its various elements have been brought to market as commodities.

Such a market system requires a degree of government intervention to ensure that certain basic principles are adhered to. Economist Jim Stanford explains that 'there is no real debate over whether governments should "intervene" in the economy: they always have, and always will. The real questions are rather different. *How* does government intervene in the economy? And in *whose* interests?'[7] In his classic treatise, *Capitalism and Freedom*, Milton Friedman made clear that government's role is to intervene on behalf of capital and, therefore, in a market system its 'major function must be to protect our freedom both from the enemies outside our gates and from our fellow-citizens: preserve law and order, to enforce private contracts, to foster competitive markets.'[8]

Friedman also argued that democracy is only attainable under a free-market economy, claiming that capitalism is 'a necessary condition for political freedom'.[9] The form of democratic governance that Friedman was referring to is a liberal democracy based upon a constitution that prioritizes individual rights, most specifically the right to private property, which translates into private ownership of the means of production. Other advocates of free-market capitalism have even defended undemocratic forms of governance so long as they maintain conditions favourable to capital. As Friedrich Hayek stated in 1981,

> At times it is necessary for a country to have, for a time, some form or other of dictatorial power. As you will understand, it is possible for a dictator to govern in a liberal way. And it is also possible for a democracy to govern with a total lack of liberalism. Personally I prefer a liberal dictator to democratic government lacking liberalism.[10]

Hayek's statement more accurately reflects the relationship between capital and democracy than does the concept of liberal democracy posited by Friedman. Ultimately, it is not important to capital whether government is democratic or not, so long as it is economically liberal, thereby facilitating capital accumulation. And while, for the most part, the free market provides capitalists with the desired freedom to generate wealth, adhering to the logic of capital often requires them to violate this ideological doctrine through the establishment of monopolies, exclusive contracts, government subsidies and tariffs, and other behaviours that contradict free-market principles when necessary to maximize profits. But Hayek's remarks do support Friedman's argument that the only form of 'democracy' that is acceptable to capital is a liberal democracy.

Von Mises, another champion of the free market, even went so far as to suggest that capitalism constitutes the ultimate economic democracy when he declared, 'The capitalistic market economy is a democracy in which every penny constitutes a vote. ... The capitalistic order, therefore, is an economic democracy in the strictest sense of the word.'[11] In one sense, Mises's definition of democracy is an accurate description of liberal democracy because every penny often does constitute a vote. However, it is not the pennies in the pockets of consumers that do the voting, as was being suggested by Mises, but rather the billions of dollars controlled by capitalist elites who use their wealth to influence political outcomes – through lobbying activities and campaign contributions. However, with regard to Mises's intended definition of economic democracy, it fails to account for those people who are too poor to be consumers of any significance. In other words, the poor have no vote in a system that prevents them from meeting their basic needs. Mises also declared that 'production is not an end in itself, its purpose is to serve consumption'.[12] Ultimately, then, in the economic democracy envisioned by Mises, those with the most pennies determine what is produced and what is consumed, which logically translates into production that serves the consumption habits of the wealthy rather than ensuring that the basic needs of all people are met.

Robert McChesney argues that the concept of democracy posited by Friedman and other advocates of capitalism has little to do with the will of the people and everything to do with protecting the freedom of certain individuals to generate wealth. According to McChesney's interpretation of this capital-friendly concept of democracy, 'Since profit-making is the essence of democracy, any government that pursues anti-market policies is anti-democratic, no matter how much informed popular support they might enjoy.'[13] This is reflected in Friedman's argument that one of government's primary roles is to protect 'our freedom both from the enemies outside our gates and from our fellow-citizens'. Since Friedman clearly linked freedom to capitalism, then his concept of democracy considers any fellow citizen who challenges the interests of capital as an 'enemy'.

Jim Stanford has also challenged Friedman's suggestion that there is an inherent link between capitalism and democracy, arguing, 'Quite the reverse: capitalism actually demonstrates a natural anti-democratic streak (by virtue of the inherent tendency for private wealth, and hence political influence, to be continually concentrated in the hands of a very small proportion of society).'[14] Ultimately, then, not only do capitalist elites possess a disproportionate degree of influence in the political sphere in a liberal democracy, but they also rule the economic realm in an authoritarian manner, with workers having no voice in the workplace. In short, under liberal democracy, political democracy exists to a degree while economic democracy does not exist at all.

The role of a liberal democracy – or a liberal dictatorship – is to ensure the existence of a system of governance that maintains a separation between the political and economic spheres by, as Friedman noted, enforcing private contracts and fostering competitive markets. Consequently, the functioning of the economy according to the logic of capital takes precedence over all other aspects of society. As Karl Polanyi explained,

> Ultimately, that is why the control of the economic system by the market is of overwhelming consequence to the whole organization of society: it means no less than the running of society as an adjunct to the market. Instead of economy being embedded in social relations, social relations are embedded in the economic system. The vital importance of the economic factor to the existence of society precludes any other result.[15]

In other words, according to the logic of capital, society exists to serve the economy, rather than the reverse. To this end, the 'rule of law' plays a crucial role in prioritizing the interests of capital under a liberal democratic system. It is the rule of law that upholds individual freedom; as Hayek noted, 'This is the classical conception of freedom under the law, a state of affairs in which a man may be coerced only where coercion is required by the general rules of law, equally applicable to all, and never by the discretionary decision of administrative authority.'[16] But these laws that are theoretically 'equally applicable to all' are based on a concept of individual rights that certain classes of people are best situated to use to their own advantage and to the disadvantage of others. Samir Amin argues that the rule of law under liberal democracy ultimately upholds private property as sacrosanct and, thereby, serves the interests of capital:

The bourgeois democracy is itself an alienated democracy. It forbids the crossing of the red line of sacrosanct property ownership. Law and money are thus inseparable. And this association accompanies the separation between the political management of society by electoral and multiparty representative democracy (where it exists) and the management of the economy which is abandoned to reason, attributed to the market. In politics citizens are equal before the law. In social reality, dominant and dominated, exploiters and exploited, are no longer equal in their capacity to make use of their rights. Social progress is exteriorised, it is not a constitutive part of the foundation of law and democracy.[17]

In essence, the individual and property rights prioritized under liberal democracy – and enforced by the rule of law – do not ensure freedom for all people, but rather maintain the conditions of inequality under which some individuals are free to exploit others. In reference to the role of the 'rule of law' in a liberal democracy to ensure that the law is 'equally applicable to all' in its protection of individual rights, Anatole France noted in 1894, 'The law, in its majestic equality, forbids the rich as well as the poor to beg in the streets, steal bread, or sleep under a bridge.'[18]

While the rule of law serves the interests of capital, Ernesto 'Che' Guevara has suggested that, under capitalism, most people's lives are even more directly impacted by a different law; one that resides at the core of capitalist logic. According to Guevara, 'In capitalist society individuals are controlled by a pitiless law usually beyond their comprehension. The alienated human specimen is tied to society as a whole by an invisible umbilical cord: the law of value. This law acts upon all aspects of one's life, shaping its course and destiny.'[19] Under this law, the value of an individual is reduced to the value of his or her role in the production process. As Mises explained,

> Man deals with other people's labor in the same way that he deals with all scarce material factors of production. He appraises it according to the principles he applies in the appraisal of all other goods. The height of wage rates is determined on the market in the

same way in which the prices of all commodities are determined. In this sense we may say that labor is a commodity.[20]

While Mises suggested that workers are free entities who possess power equal to that of capital in a free market, Karl Marx and Friedrich Engels argued that capitalism has little to do with freedom for workers – the overwhelming majority of people – and more to do with creating conditions that permit capital to exploit these 'human' commodities as it does all other commodities in its never-ending drive to maximize profits. Consequently, they explained, under a global free-market economy, capital

> has resolved personal worth into exchange value, and in place of the numberless indefeasible chartered freedoms, has set up that single, unconscionable freedom – Free Trade. In one word, for exploitation, veiled by religious and political illusions, it has substituted naked, shameless, direct, brutal exploitation. ... The need of a constantly expanding market for its products chases the bourgeoisie over the entire surface of the globe. It must nestle everywhere, settle everywhere, establish connexions everywhere.[21]

And thus capital is compelled to exploit both labour and natural resources throughout the globe. Marx noted that there are two principal acts involved in capital's expansion: production and circulation. He argued that capital's drive to increase surplus value (i.e. profits and other capital gains) through the expansion of the production of commodities also requires an increase in circulation – and a corresponding increase in consumption of the commodities in circulation. Therefore, as Marx noted, 'a precondition of production based on capital is therefore *the production of a constantly widening sphere of circulation*'.[22] There are three scenarios in which capital can increase circulation: population growth, an expansion of markets, and the increased social needs of workers (i.e. as consumers).

Capital's need to expand over 'the entire surface of the globe' to exploit workers and natural resources and to gain access to new markets actually constitutes a direct inversion of the traditional concept of dependency theory. Capital's inherent need to constantly expand – and the corresponding drain of wealth from the global South to support the relatively luxurious lifestyles enjoyed in the global North – has resulted in nations in the North becoming increasingly dependent on the cheap labour and natural resources of the South.[23] As David Harvey has argued,

> Access to cheaper inputs is, therefore, just as important as access to widening markets in keeping profitable opportunities open. The implication is that non-capitalist territories should be forced open not only to trade (which could be helpful) but also to permit capital to invest in profitable ventures using cheaper labour power, raw materials, low-cost land, and the like. The general thrust of any capitalistic logic of power is not that territories should be held back from capitalist development, but that they should be continuously opened up.[24]

This continuous opening up of territory has created great wealth at the core of the global capitalist system – the global North – and mass immiseration on the periphery – the global South. As a result of capital's inherent drive to expand, inequality has increased dramatically with the wealth gap between the global North and the global South growing from a factor of 3:1 in 1820 to 35:1 in 1950 and to 72:1 in 1990.[25] Indian physicist and philosopher Vandana Shiva explains how capital's historic drive to widen the spheres of production and circulation in order to accumulate resulted in this trend of growing inequality:

> The poor are not those who have been 'left behind'; they are the ones who have been robbed. The riches accumulated by Europe are based on riches taken from Asia, Africa and Latin America. Without the destruction of India's rich textile industry, without the takeover of the spice trade, without the genocide of the native American tribes, without Africa's slavery, the Industrial Revolution would not have led to new riches for Europe or the U.S. It was this violent takeover of Third World resources and markets that created wealth in the North and poverty in the South.[26]

Shiva claims that this process, what Marx termed 'primitive accumulation', is driven by capital's inherent drive to expand

and to generate economic growth. The problem, notes Shiva, is that this requires the commodification of virtually everything. In other words, nothing has value until it enters the market. Shiva points out that under capitalism 'if you consume what you produce, you do not really produce, at least not economically speaking. If I grow my own food, and do not sell it, then this does not contribute to GDP, and so does not contribute towards "growth".'[27] Consequently, under the logic of capital, those who engage in traditional and sustainable modes of production must be incorporated – often through coercion – into the ever-widening spheres of production and circulation. As Shiva explains,

> For centuries, living according to principles of sustenance has given human societies the material basis for survival. Limits in nature have been respected and have guided the limits of human consumption. When society's relationship with nature is based on sustenance, nature exists as a commons. It only becomes a resource when profit becomes the organising principle and creates a financial imperative for the exploitation of this 'resource' for the market.[28]

Milton Friedman defended capital's practice of primitive accumulation by referring to the enclosing of the 'commons' in Britain as an example of the benefits of such a process. Between 1760 and 1815, the British Parliament passed a series of Enclosure Acts that ultimately resulted in the enclosure, or privatization, of commonly held lands that constituted 21 per cent of English territory.[29] The implementation of the Enclosure Acts prevented much of the rural population from engaging in the generations-old practice of grazing their animals and cultivating their crops on commonly held lands, thereby forcing them to move to the cities in search of jobs. Friedman argued that the depressing depiction of working life in the cities of Victorian-era Britain has been presented out of context. According to Friedman, 'What happens in the picture that's drawn of Britain in the nineteenth century is that there is no image of what went before. Why is it that all these people from the farming, from the rural, areas came into the city? Did they come to the city because they thought it would be worse? Or because they thought it would be better? And was it worse or was it better?'[30] Obviously, people moved to the city because they thought it would be better than life in the country-side. But Friedman was not being intellectually honest in the way he presented his argument. After all, most farmers that moved to the city did so because they had no choice. The privatization of the commons forced them to migrate to the cities and become wage labourers in the textile mills and other emerging industries. In other words, a life of squalor in the cities was preferable to starvation in the countryside. As Kovel explains,

> One prevailing theme of the Commons is that it is 'enclosed' by the march of the formal, class-bound economy. This has a two-fold meaning: that the people of the Commons, that is, the primary producers of society, are forcibly separated from their means of production; and that the rulers are made richer by the enclosing. In other words, closing the Commons means both the robbery and the alienation of the original people, as part of the creation of private property; it is the precondition for the 'primitive accumulation' of capital, and is continually reproduced in capital's invasions. Note, too, that enclosure made commoners into 'free' laborers, free to go to the city, free to live in appalling poverty and filth, free to become proletarians and sub-proletarians in the rising regime of capital, a process that still obtains throughout capital's ecumene.[31]

It was essential for capital that the commons be enclosed and that private property be made sacrosanct. And it was inter-ventions by a liberal democratic government on behalf of capital that facilitated this process in Britain. The enclosures constituted the first stage of accumulation, which created the conditions conducive to further accumulation through industrial produc-tion. As historian Donald Leech notes, the

> parliamentary enclosures signified the final transition to the capi-talist economy.... as elites appropriated the commons a struggle began between the idea of the common and of self interest. From the nineteenth century to today the successful process of turning all land into private production in the name of mutual self interest has been claimed by political economists and historians as inevitable and progressive.[32]

THE NEOLIBERAL ERA

Over the past few decades, neoliberal globalization has intensified the pace with which capital, in the name of 'progress', has geographically widened both its spheres of production and circulation through the process of what David Harvey has called 'accumulation by dispossession'. It achieved this by dismantling the Fordist compact and the broader Keynesian policy framework that were established during the middle decades of the twentieth century and that permitted organized labour in the global North to garner a greater share of surplus value.

The Keynesian policy framework has been called a mixed economy, but according to Ludwig von Mises,

> The market economy or capitalism, as it is usually called, and the socialist economy preclude one another. There is no mixture of the two systems possible or thinkable; there is no such thing as a mixed economy ... If within a society based on private ownership of the means of production some of these means are publicly owned and operated – that is, owned and operated by the government or one of its agencies – this does not make for a mixed system which would combine socialism and capitalism. The fact that the state or municipalities own and operate some plants does not alter the characteristic features of the market economy. The publicly owned and operated enterprises are subject to the sovereignty of the market.[33]

The contemporary role played by China's state-owned companies in the global economy is a perfect illustration of the point made by Mises. While state-owned companies may increase the revenues of a national government and help facilitate a moderate redistribution of the national wealth, they are still reliant on success in the global market for their survival – and that success requires adhering to the logic of capital.

During the Keynesian era, reductions in inequality were achieved within many nations in the global North, but the wealth that was redistributed domestically remained predicated in large part on a neocolonial capitalist system, and any nation that dared to challenge the interests of capital quickly incurred the wrath of the United States, as people in Iran, Guatemala, Cuba, Indonesia, Chile and Nicaragua, among others, can attest. Also troubling, with regard to the Keynesian model, was its failure to slow capital's onslaught against nature.

Social democrats often hold up Sweden as an example because, despite the introduction of certain neoliberal policies, it has largely managed to preserve the social programmes it implemented during the Keynesian era. Often ignored, however, is the fact that Sweden's social democracy has depended on imperialism to garner sufficient wealth to distribute more equally among its population in order to attain impressive social indicators and a high standard of living. After all, Sweden is home to hundreds of multinational companies and is the world's tenth-largest arms exporter.[34]

Ultimately, capital was willing to tolerate the Keynesian policy framework in the context of the shadow cast by the Great Depression and the appeal of the Soviet 'socialist' alternative because, as Mises noted, the market remained the principal arbiter of economic activity and profit generation was robust during much of that period. But as soon as the rate of economic growth slowed in the global North, resulting in capital experiencing a crisis of accumulation, it became necessary for capital to dismantle the Keynesian policy framework in order to resume expansion, this time under neoliberal globalization. Capital viewed the higher wages achieved by workers in the global North under the Fordist compact and the Keynesian policy framework as a barrier to overcome in order to recapture for itself a greater share of surplus value. Ultimately, the redistributive project under the Keynesian policy framework proved unsustainable because it contradicted the internal logic of capital and was implemented under liberal democratic regimes that ultimately served the interests of capital.

According to Samir Amin, the triple failure of the regulated social models – the Keynesian welfare state in the West, 'actually existing socialism' in the East and popular nationalism in the global South – during the second half of the twentieth

century made it possible for capital to consolidate once again
its hegemony over the global economy.[35] The resulting shift
towards a global free-market economy in the latter decades of the
twentieth century provided capital with the conditions necessary
to expand its access to cheap labour, raw materials and new
markets in the global South; it also allowed for a renewed assault
on the 'commons'.

Under neoliberal globalization, capital has succeeded in its efforts to widen the spheres of production and circulation by utilizing the policies implemented by powerful national governments
– particularly the United States – and international institutions
such as the World Trade Organization (WTO), the International
Monetary Fund (IMF) and the World Bank. In essence, these
international institutions constitute a form of 'liberal' government at the international level while their regulations serve as
the 'rule of law' by which national governments must abide. These
new imperialist structures, like the old ones under European
colonialism, are reliant on the existence of political and economic
elites in positions of power within nations of the global South who
can work domestically to ensure that their governments adhere to
the dictates of capital. And if domestic ruling elites in the global
South waver in their commitment to capital – or fail to maintain
control over the masses – then economic sanctions or military
intervention are initiated in order to restore the natural order
of things, as evidenced by the ongoing US economic embargo
against Cuba and the US invasions of Panama and Iraq among
others. Perhaps most illustrative of this new imperialist order
under neoliberal globalization in the post-Cold War era is the
increasingly prominent role of NATO in military interventions
beyond its original North Atlantic sphere of influence.[36]

These international institutions have been at the forefront of
implementing neoliberal globalization, which has allowed capital
to increase dramatically its share of surplus value in recent
decades, as evidenced by soaring stock market indexes and the
record profits posted by many of the world's largest corporations.
However, much of the profit generated under neoliberalism does

not result from the production of goods; it is 'fictitious', and
further illustrates the inherent need of capital to expand by
whatever means possible.

The unilateral delinking of the dollar from the gold standard by
the Nixon administration in the 1970s and the ensuing deregulation of financial markets under neoliberalism have resulted in a
series of financial crises over the past few decades. The most serious of these crises struck in 2008, initiating a global depression in
which the peoples of the global South have been the hardest hit.
But in the midst of this economic crisis, capital remained awash
in money it desperately needed to invest in order to accumulate
further. The global depression, however, had reduced consumer
demand for goods, thereby slowing economic growth throughout
the world. So what did capital do with all this money burning a
hole in its pocket? It invested in itself. Companies began spending
billions of dollars to purchase their own stock and to buy out their
competitors; activities that do not increase production or create
jobs, but do achieve capital accumulation. One such example was
the attempt by Australian mining giant BHP Billiton to purchase
Canada's Potash Corporation. After its takeover bid failed, BHP
Billiton instead purchased its own shares as a means of disposing
of its cash.[37] As financial analyst Don Pittis explains,

> From the viewpoint of a company, buying another company or
> buying its own shares might help it get rid of cash. It is not investing
> in the old-fashioned sense where an entrepreneur creates a business
> from nothing. It is not even like the business mentioned above that
> invests in new plant and equipment to expand its business. Instead,
> it is just a matter of bidding up existing assets. The total amount of
> economic activity doesn't change, only the price of the assets.[38]

And so, while hundreds of millions of people were being
forced to endure poverty, hunger and even death as a result of
the global economic crisis, the internal logic of capital prevented
the system from addressing these very real human needs. Instead,
capital continued on its drive to accumulate, this time through
cannibalistic practices.

Capital's other response to the bursting of its financial bubble in 2008 was to reinflate the bubble through an even greater expansion of both credit and debt in a desperate effort to maintain a system that has reached the point of permanent crisis. As John Holloway explains,

> The onset of crisis gives rise to an expansion of credit and debt. Accumulation becomes more and more fictitious: the monetary representation of value becomes more and more detached from the value actually produced. Capitalism becomes more fictitious, more make-believe: workers make believe that their income is greater than it is; capitalists make believe that their businesses are profitable; banks make believe that the debtors are financially sound. All make believe that there is a greater production of surplus value than is actually the case.[39]

While so-called fictitious capitalism has gained prominence under neoliberal globalization, the process of accumulation by dispossession has continued in conjunction with capital's financial Ponzi scheme. Millions of people continue to be displaced from the countryside to the cities, where only a small percentage manage to obtain formal-sector jobs in the manufacturing or service sectors while the majority are forced to survive by engaging in the informal economy. But under neoliberal globalization, capital in its drive to accumulate through dispossession has sought to enclose a much broader 'commons' than that simply related to land. As Harvey notes,

> All the features of primitive accumulation that Marx mentions have remained powerfully present within capitalism's historical geography up until now. Displacement of peasant populations and the formation of a landless proletariat has accelerated in countries such as Mexico and India in the last three decades, many formerly common property resources, such as water, have been privatized (often at World Bank insistence) and brought within the capitalist logic of accumulation, alternative (indigenous and even, in the case of the United States, petty commodity) forms of production and consumption have been suppressed. Nationalized industries have been privatized. Family farming has been taken over by agribusiness. And slavery has not disappeared (particularly in the sex trade).[40]

In addition to the privatization of public-owned entities referred to by Harvey, the collapse of the Soviet Union and its integration, along with China, into the global capitalist system have also provided crucial outlets that have permitted capital to expand its spheres of production and circulation.

Capital's expansion under neoliberal globalization has not been restricted to the dispossession and privatization of physical entities such as land and publicly owned companies; it has extended into the immaterial world of intellectual 'property'. Under the WTO's intellectual property rights regime, corporations have been allowed to patent agricultural seeds, medicines and knowledge that were traditionally considered to be a commons freely accessible to all peoples.

The enclosing of the commons – in its various forms – and the undermining of traditional modes of agricultural production are intentional outcomes of policies imposed on peoples of the global South by powerful nations in the North and international institutions serving the interests of capital. The aggregate effect of these policies benefits capital, primarily based in the global North, and disadvantages small farmers, the majority of whom are in the global South. Small rural producers are forced to abandon their lands and to become wage labourers – and consumers – in the cities. According to Marx,

> The expropriation of the agricultural producer, of the peasant, from the soil, is the basis of the whole [capitalist] process. The history of this expropriation assumes different aspects in different countries, and runs through its various phases in different orders of succession, and at different historical epochs.[41]

Kovel's description of how this process of expropriation of sustainable communities in the global South has most commonly been carried out under neoliberalism is particularly instructive:

> Typically ... what breaks up the life-world of tribal society is some encroachment upon the land. With the productive foundation of society interrupted, a complex and disintegrative chain of events

is set in motion. As old ways no longer make sense, a kind of desire is set loose; and as this is now relatively shapeless and boundless, the virus of capital, with its promise of limitless wealth and godlike transformation, is able to take hold. This is generally accompanied by the mass-cultural invasion that encodes capital's logos in the form of commodities. Once 'Coca-Cola, the real thing,' replaces traditional reality, the internal colonization that perfects the takeover of peripheral societies is well under way.[42]

The process of accumulation by dispossession, in conjunction with technological advances, leads to a centralization of wealth in the hands of the capitalist class and a diminished share of surplus value for workers, thereby increasing inequality. Consequently, notes Galtung,

> Capitalism is a system pumping wealth from the poor, up to the rich, with a tiny trickle down if there are no counter-measures. The net result is obvious: poverty, even misery at the bottom of national and global economies with wealth accumulating in rich countries and rich people, and particularly in rich people in the rich countries.[43]

Ultimately, as Marx pointed out, capital requires fewer and fewer workers because

> it is capitalist accumulation itself that constantly produces, and produces indeed in direct relation with its own energy and extent, a relatively redundant working population, i.e. a population which is superfluous to capital's average requirements for its own valorization, and is therefore a surplus population.[44]

The 'redundant working population' referred to by Marx consists, in the twenty-first century, of hundreds of millions of people throughout the global South who are struggling to survive in the informal sector. Their numbers far exceed that required by capital to serve as an effective army of surplus labour in order to keep wages low in the formal sector. This redundant working population is a consequence of the displacement of the rural population from its traditional lifestyles, which has driven the process of urbanization in the global South over the past half-century. However, unlike the previous enclosure processes that occurred in Britain and other Western European nations, where many people forced into the cities eventually gained access to factory jobs, much of the global South has experienced urbanization without industrialization. According to Mike Davis, the process of neoliberal globalization has been largely responsible for this phenomenon because its 'policies of agricultural deregulation and fiscal discipline enforced by the IMF and World Bank continued to generate an exodus of surplus rural labor to urban slums even as cities ceased to be job machines'.[45]

According to the United Nations, the percentage of economically active population in the global South engaged in the informal sector has almost doubled in recent decades from 21 per cent in 1970 to approximately 40 per cent.[46] The lack of formal-sector employment has forced people to engage in a desperate struggle for economic survival in the cities, which has contributed to increased levels of crime and violence in what Davis has called 'the daily violence of economic exclusion'.[47]

By turning people engaged in traditional and sustainable agricultural practices in virtually every corner of the world into wage labourers, capital has also sought to widen its sphere of circulation by increasing the social needs of these workers. But it is in this process that the inherent contradiction in capitalism referred to by Marx becomes apparent. Capital's need to drive down wages in order to increase surplus value through ever-higher levels of production and lower wages conflicts with the ability of workers to consume at a sufficient rate the ever-increasing number of goods produced. Furthermore, technological advances allow capital to produce at ever-greater levels of efficiency with fewer and fewer workers – and, by logical extension, fewer and fewer consumers. Consequently, as Marx explained, there is 'a constant tension between the restricted dimensions of consumption on the capitalist basis, and a production that is constantly striving to overcome these immanent barriers', with the result being '*overproduction*, the fundamental contradiction of developed capital'.[48]

In short, increasing numbers of the world's population are no longer of any use to capital because hi-tech production methods render them redundant as producers and poverty precludes them as consumers. According to philosopher Slavoj Žižek,

> As some social analysts and economists have suggested, the con-temporary explosion of economic productivity confronts us with the ultimate case of the [80-20] rule: the coming global economy will tend towards a state in which only 20 per cent of the labor force are able to do all the necessary work, so that 80 per cent of people will be basically irrelevant and of no use, thus potentially unemployed. As this logic reaches its extreme, would it not be reasonable to bring it to its self-negation: is not a system which renders 80 per cent of the people irrelevant and useless *itself irrelevant and of no use?*[49]

Ultimately, despite more than half a century of loans and foreign development aid, not a single so-called Third World nation has become a First World nation since the end of World War II.[50] The international structures under neoliberal global-ization ensure that nations of the global South are perpetually 'developing' and that they never actually become 'developed'. Under neoliberal globalization, the imperialist nations in the global North have ensured capital's continued dominance over the peoples of the global South in what sociologist William I. Robinson has called a world war being waged by a rich and power-ful minority against the global poor in which 'casualties already number in the hundreds of millions, and threaten to mount into the billions ... the level of social conflict and human destruction is reaching bellicose proportions'.[51] Consequently, claims Amin, 'The dominant class at the world level ... has become the enemy of all humanity.'[52]

CONCLUSION

As we have seen, the logic of capital requires the continuous expansion of the spheres of both production and circulation. As a result, according to Antonio Negri, 'Capital has conquered and enveloped the entire life-world, its hegemony is global....

We are completely immersed in the world of "exchange value" and its brutal and ferocious reality.'[53] This process of capital accumulation has been premissed on the dispossession of peasants throughout the world. It has also required the commodification of virtually everything and everyone in order to generate wealth for a minority. Clearly, the capitalist system is dependent on a process of exploitation and oppression that results in social injustice and inequality – in both power and wealth. In reference to capital's inherent need to generate inequality, Marx noted,

> It makes an accumulation of misery a necessary condition, corresponding to the accumulation of wealth. Accumulation of wealth at one pole is, therefore, at the same time accumulation of misery, the torment of labour, slavery, ignorance, brutalization and moral degradation at the opposite pole.[54]

Every day, hundreds of millions of people throughout the global South struggle to meet their fundamental needs – with many failing to do so. Meanwhile, a small minority accumulate great wealth. Such social injustices and inequality are inherent components of capitalism; as such, they constitute structural violence. In fact, as philosopher István Mészáros notes, '*Structurally enforced inequality* is the all-important defining characteristic of the capital system, without which it could not function for a single day.'[55] But while it is evident that structural violence is inherent in the internal logic of capital, does it constitute structural genocide?

3

STRUCTURAL GENOCIDE:
THE CASES OF MEXICO AND INDIA

> Poverty is the worst form of violence.
>
> *Mohandas K. Gandhi*

Much of the focus on politically motivated genocide and mass killings has highlighted those gross atrocities perpetrated by leaders of various 'communist' regimes, such as Stalin in the Soviet Union and Pol Pot in Cambodia. But similar instances of genocide and mass killings have also occurred under fascism (Hitler in Germany) and capitalism (the annihilation of the indigenous peoples of the Americas, the deaths of Africans in the slave trade, and the killings perpetrated by military governments in Argentina, Chile, Guatemala, El Salvador and other countries in Latin America during the 1970s and 1980s, to list just a few).

In each of the communist cases – as well as in the fascist example – the principal perpetrator, either through direct physical violence or structural violence, was a single tyrannical leader. However, unlike in the cases of Stalin and Pol Pot, structural violence under capitalism does not have an easily identifiable face, precisely because it is systemic. Echoing Galtung's point about the anonymity of structural violence, Slavoj Žižek argues that the systemic violence inherent in capitalism is much more uncanny than any direct capitalist socio-ideological violence: this violence is no longer attributable to concrete individuals and their 'evil' intentions, but is purely 'objective,' systemic, anonymous. ... Our blindness to the results of systemic violence is perhaps most clearly perceptible in debates about communist crimes. Responsibility for communist crimes is easy to allocate; we are dealing with subjective evil, with agents who did wrong. We can even identify the ideological sources of the crimes – totalitarian ideology, *The Communist Manifesto*, Rousseau, even Plato. But when one draws attention to the millions who died as the result of capitalist globalisation, from the tragedy of Mexico in the sixteenth century through to the Belgian Congo holocaust a century ago, responsibility is largely denied. All this seems just to have happened as the result of an 'objective' process, which nobody planned and executed and for which there was no 'Capitalist Manifesto'.[1]

For the most part, the political group or collectivity that is the victim of the structural violence inherent in capitalism consists of the billions of peasants in the global South who remain dependent on agriculture for their survival and the billions of slum-dwellers who have already been dispossessed of their lands and who are struggling to survive in the informal sector. In other words, the lower classes, or the working classes, in the broadest sense of the term, are the principal victims. Therefore the structural violence inherent in capitalism is clearly class-based; targeting a particular socio-economic stratum marked by race and gender characteristics, but with the common denominator among all of the victims being their relationship to the dominant modes of production under capitalism.

The following case studies will illustrate how the structural violence inherent in capitalism is manifesting itself in the early twenty-first century. Ultimately, these cases make apparent that structural violence is occurring in genocidal proportions in the global South under capitalism. The first case involves the forced displacement of Mexican farmers from their lands under the North American Free Trade Agreement (NAFTA). While it could be argued that the scale of deaths in Mexico does not constitute genocide, they clearly illustrate how the structural violence in

that nation and others in the global South constitutes a component of the broader structural genocide occurring globally. The
second examines the farmer suicide crisis in India resulting
from neoliberal globalization. The final case (examined in the
ensuing chapter) analyses the deaths that result from hunger and
from preventable and treatable diseases due to the profit motive
inherent in capitalism. The magnitude of deaths in each of the
cases of India and sub-Saharan Africa represents an instance of
structural genocide of itself, as well as constituting a component
of the broader structural genocide.

Each of these cases illustrates uniquely different ways in which
structural violence manifests itself. They also make evident that
the victims are not only those who die as a result of structural
violence. After all, discussions about the Nazi Holocaust do not
begin and end with those who died in the concentration camps;
they often include the stories of those who were interned but
survived the genocide – they too were victims of the violence.
Similarly, the victims of the structural violence inherent in
capitalism do not solely consist of the tens of millions around
the world who die annually, but also those who survive – or find
a way to exist within – the structural violence to which they are
subjected.

FORCED DISPLACEMENT IN MEXICO

On 1 January 1994, the North American Free Trade Agreement
(NAFTA) between the United States, Canada and Mexico came
into effect, constituting yet another attempt by capital to expand
its spheres of production and circulation. Not coincidentally, on
that same day an armed uprising by indigenous peoples in the
southern Mexican state of Chiapas took place. The indigenous
protesters, officially called the Zapatista Army of National Lib-
eration (EZLN), but more commonly known as the Zapatistas,
chose that specific day to rise up in order to protest against
NAFTA, particularly its impacts on the agricultural sector, and
the Mexican government's related decision to repeal Article 27

of the Constitution, which had permitted communal land titles for indigenous peoples.

The intent of NAFTA was to create a free market for many agricultural and manufactured goods that transcended the borders of the three participating nations. The free movement of labour, however, was not part of the agreement. Even though labour is deemed to be a commodity under capitalism, workers do not possess the same rights to free movement under NAFTA as other commodities. Ultimately, NAFTA is far from a free-trade agreement, not only due to its restrictions on the movement of workers, but also because it allows for so-called artificial trade barriers that favour corporations, particularly US agribusinesses.

NAFTA has dramatically reduced the amounts of tariffs and quotas that a government can apply to imports from a NAFTA partner. However, it still permits agricultural subsidies, largely at the insistence of the US government.[2] Therefore NAFTA permits the three governments to provide subsidies to their agricultural producers. In reality, however, the United States and Canada can provide subsidies, but Mexico cannot. The reason for the discrepancy rests in the broader neoliberal framework of global capitalism. Conditions placed on loans provided to Mexico by both the IMF and the United States required that the Mexican government reduce its subsidies to the agricultural sector. As Steve Suppan explains, 'Subsidies of basic foodstuffs were among the public expenditures slashed to achieve macro-economic objectives stipulated in the February 1995 U.S–Mexico loan agreement and in the loan Letter of Intent with the IMF.'[3] Therefore, while NAFTA permitted Mexico to subsidize its agricultural sector, neoliberal austerity measures imposed on the country through loan agreements ensured that Mexico would not be able to subsidize its agricultural sector to the same degree as the United States and Canada.

The biased structure in favour of agribusinesses based in the United States and Canada constitutes structural violence that has devastated the lives of millions of Mexican small farmers. NAFTA has resulted in the dumping of heavily subsidized food products by

US agribusinesses onto the Mexican market – the most devastating of which has been corn, the principal food staple in Mexico. Between 1997 and 2005, US agricultural subsidies to domestic corn producers averaged $4.5 billion a year.[4] This allowed US agribusinesses to export corn to Mexico and to sell it for less than what it would have cost to produce if production were not subsidized. Not surprisingly, unsubsidized Mexican farmers could not compete with the imported subsidized US corn, and imports from the United States quickly came to dominate the Mexican market, increasing by 413 per cent over pre-NAFTA levels.[5] As a result of the disparity in subsidies, it is estimated that Mexican producers of corn, wheat, rice, cotton and soybeans have lost more than $1 billion a year in earnings under NAFTA.[6]

For proponents of NAFTA, this scenario is not necessarily problematic. As Suppan notes, 'According to the theory of "comparative advantage" touted by NAFTA proponents, Mexico would be able to import basic grains more cheaply than it could produce them.'[7] And this was certainly true, although only because of the subsidies provided to US agribusinesses. Those Mexican farmers who could no longer compete would, in theory, abandon agriculture and become wage labourers in Mexico's manufacturing sector and begin purchasing imported food. And Mexican farmers did abandon their lands; in fact they abandoned them in startling numbers. By 2006, it was estimated that as many as 2 million Mexican farmers had quit farming.[8] And since the World Bank reported that the rural poverty rate in Mexico had reached 82 per cent by 1998, those peasants who had been forced to abandon farming had little choice but to head to the cities in search of work.[9] Meanwhile, multinational corporations gained ownership of much of the abandoned farmland, some of which was indigenous land that was no longer protected under the recently repealed Article 27 of the Mexican Constitution.[10]

Some Mexicans chose to fight capital's expansion of its spheres of production and circulation under NAFTA. When the Zapatistas took up arms in 1994, they sought to ignite a national uprising

in order to seize state power. When the national uprising failed
to materialize, the Zapatistas switched their focus to the gaining of autonomy for their communities in the Lacandón Jungle
in Chiapas. While the Zapatistas have established impressive
examples of participatory democracy at the community level
and have made some social gains, particularly in the provision
of prenatal health care to expectant mothers, they are nevertheless under increasing threat from capital.[11] Zapatista communities are surrounded by constantly expanding mining and
oil exploration, agrofuel production and so-called ecotourism
initiatives that threaten the quasi-autonomy the Zapatistas have
enjoyed over the past fifteen years.[12] Consequently, while many
activists laud the Zapatista uprising as the first 'post-modern
revolution' because of its attempts to initiate radical change at
the grassroots level without seizing state power, the struggle
could just as easily be viewed as an illustration of the limitations
inherent in attempting to create an alternative society within
broader capitalist structures. After all, under NAFTA's favourable
investment conditions, US and Canadian mining companies have
displaced thousands of peasants and gained control over more
than a million hectares of land in the state of Chiapas.[13]

While the Zapatistas fought against NAFTA, many of Mexico's
displaced peasants joined the exodus of poor people from various
parts of the country to cities in northern Mexico that were experiencing a boom in the manufacturing sector during the early years
of the trade agreement. By 2000, NAFTA had created 700,000
manufacturing jobs in *maquiladoras*, or assembly plants, and
the massive displacement of peasants from the countryside to
the cities ensured a sufficient army of surplus labour to keep
wages low – an average of $1.74 an hour.[14] But by 2003, more than
300,000 of those jobs had moved overseas, primarily to China,
where the interests of capital were being better served through
labour costs that were even lower than in Mexico.[15]

Even at its height, NAFTA failed to create enough new
manufacturing jobs to accommodate the newly displaced
peasant population. Furthermore, many of the new jobs created

simply replaced existing manufacturing jobs that were lost due to NAFTA. It is estimated that during the first decade of the free-trade agreement some 28,000 small and medium-sized businesses shut down because of their inability to compete with the cheap consumer products being imported and sold by multinational companies such as Wal-Mart that had begun operating in Mexico.[16] Ultimately, total manufacturing employment throughout the country declined to 3.5 million by 2004, from a high of 4.1 million in 2000.[17]

The displacement of peasants in Mexico has paralleled a similar process throughout Latin America where farmers are impacted not only by neoliberal agricultural policies, but also by the opening up of natural resources to multinational corporations, particularly in the oil and mining sectors. Throughout the region, indigenous communities are engaged in a struggle to preserve their traditional – and often sustainable – ways of life against multinational mining companies that seek to exploit the natural resources situated in their territories. In almost every country in which these struggles are occurring, the mining companies are backed by liberal democratic governments that see foreign investment and the unsustainable exploitation of natural resources as essential for achieving economic growth.

Colombia has been Latin America's neoliberal poster child over the past decade and its economic growth has been driven by the exploitation of the country's natural resources, particularly oil, coal and gold, by foreign companies. With some 4 million internal refugees, Colombia has the second largest internally displaced population in the world, after the Sudan.[18] Many have been forced from their lands by direct physical violence related to the country's armed conflict – often by the Colombian military and right-wing paramilitary groups serving the interests of multinational corporations. However, many others have become economic refugees due to the structural violence inherent in neoliberal policies that has dispossessed them of their lands in order to facilitate capital accumulation for foreign companies.[19] Whereas 31 per cent of Colombia's displaced families lived in

poverty before they were forced from their lands, that number
rose to 81 per cent when they became refugees.[20]

The process of accumulation by dispossession drives many
peasants to the cities, where their lack of education and job
skills leaves them no option but to struggle to survive in the
informal sector. In the first decade of the twenty-first century, 57
per cent of the economically active population in Latin America
existed in the informal sector, which also accounted for four out
of every five new 'jobs'. In fact, according to Mike Davis, 'the
only jobs created in Mexico between 2000 and 2004 were in
the informal sector.'[21]

One economic option for unemployed Mexican workers in the
border region is to become engaged in the illicit drug trade.
Mexican drug cartels have become dominant players in the
trafficking of cocaine and other illicit drugs into the United
States. As one financial analyst stated,

> NAFTA has greatly strengthened the drug cartels, which thrive on
> social instability ... the displaced population in northern Mexico
> couldn't go back to their farming jobs, so they saw the drug trade
> as their only economic opportunity. That's why the second biggest
> export and industry in Mexico is the drug trade, after oil production.
> Supplied with a limitless pool of desperate, unemployed recruits, the
> cartels have taken advantage of increased truck flows through the
> US border to make Mexico the main smuggling conduit for Andean
> cocaine. The trade is worth at least US$50 billion a year.[22]

The turf wars being waged between Mexico's drug cartels,
as well as the battles being fought between the cartels and the
Mexican army, have resulted in skyrocketing murder rates, particularly in northern Mexico. The violence has not only impacted
those involved in the drug trade. The social instability has made
it increasingly difficult for the general population to avoid getting
caught up in violence related to an industry that thrives off the
economic desperation of impoverished Mexicans. In 2010, the
carnage reached new levels when 15,273 people were killed in
drug-related violence, bringing the total number of deaths in the

four years since President Felipe Calderón launched a crackdown on the cartels to 34,612.[23]

Not coincidently, the growth of the Mexican drug cartels and the related increase in violence followed on the heels of US drug war 'victories' in Colombia that dismantled the two dominant cocaine cartels in that South American nation. In essence, the dismantling of the two cartels and the militarization of the war on drugs under Plan Colombia have simply shifted the centre of drug-trafficking operations – and drug violence – from Colombia to organized crime groups in Mexico. The United States has once again responded with a militaristic counter-narcotics plan called the Merida Initiative, which has been dubbed Plan Mexico. Ultimately, the structural violence inherent in capitalism, which has forcibly dispossessed Mexican peasants of their lands and livelihoods, has evolved into direct physical violence perpetrated against tens of thousands of people who have found themselves caught up in the escalating drug war.

In addition to drug-related violence is the femicide that is occurring along the border, particularly in the city of Juárez. The emergence of maquiladora work in border cities in the mid-1990s not only attracted displaced peasants; it also proved to be a magnet for tens of thousands of impoverished young women from throughout Mexico. In fact, most of the maquiladora jobs created under NAFTA have been filled by young women, who are forced to endure sexual harassment as well as management's anti-union attitudes. According to sociologist Leslie Salzinger, the hiring process favours young women under 20 years of age who have a 'sexualized body type' and who are childless, not pregnant and are on birth control.[24] These sexist hiring practices inevitably lead to a sexually charged environment on the shop floor between male supervisors and female workers. As Salzinger notes,

> Supervisors not only use their position in production for sexual access, they also use a highly sexualized discourse around work-ers as a means of labor control. It is striking to watch them wan-dering their lines, monitoring efficiency and legs simultaneously – their gaze focused sometimes on fingers at work, sometimes on

the nail polish that adorns them. Often supervisors will stop by a favorite operator – chatting, checking quality, flirting. Their approval marks 'good worker' and 'desirable woman' in a single gesture.[25]

The sexually charged atmosphere, and the corresponding sexual harassment, in the maquiladoras quickly transcended the workplace and began to permeate the culture of border cities such as Juárez. This has manifested itself in the most brutal manner imaginable with an estimated 800 women, many of them maquiladora workers, having been murdered in Juárez since NAFTA was implemented. The current murder rate in Juárez of 23 per 100,000 women is three times the rate that the World Health Organization (WHO) defines as an epidemic and more than double that prior to NAFTA.[26] While there is no proof of a causal relation between NAFTA and the increased rate of murders of women, the evidence suggests that some sort of correlation between the two exists.

The implementation of NAFTA expanded the already-existing hegemony of capital in Mexico. It has also intensified the process of social breakdown that results from dispossessing people of their sole means of subsistence and has contributed to increased levels of direct physical violence. Kovel highlights some of the elements that have been factors in the social chaos prevalent in Mexico's border cities:

[The] decay of religion, narco-trafficking, promiscuously available assault weapons, gangs (an estimated 250 in Juárez) arising from society's breakup and become a law until themselves [sic], along with the breakup of moral systems that comes from having a superpower suck a society's blood with instruments like NAFTA and the *maquiladora*, all played upon by capital's ever-present culture of commodified desire and eroticism. There is a nihilism that brings out the predatory remorseless killing potential in human beings, bred in conditions of extreme alienation such as appears in the surging world megacities – Lagos, Nairobi, Mumbai, Djakarta, and Manila – where those tossed up by globalized capital try to reconstruct life in appalling circumstances.[27]

Given the devastating economic impacts of NAFTA on millions of Mexicans and the resulting social instability and related criminal violence, it is no surprise that the emergence of the so-called illegal immigrant problem in the United States coincided with the implementation of the free-trade agreement. NAFTA's displacement of peasants and its failure to provide them with viable economic alternatives has forced millions of people to seek their economic survival elsewhere, and the most logical destination for many is the United States. Throughout much of the twentieth century, the migration of Mexicans to the United States constituted little more than a trickle. As a result, there were only 4.8 million Mexican-born residents in the United States in 1994, the year that NAFTA came into effect. By 2000, that number had almost doubled to 9 million, and it continued to grow after that with more than 600,000 Mexicans crossing the border in 2002 alone.[28] Many of these immigrants who had crossed the increasingly militarized border were 'illegals'. Not surprisingly, entrepreneurs quickly devised ways of profiting from Mexico's social crisis by engaging in human trafficking, sometimes with fatal consequences for the economic refugees. According to US government statistics, more than 2,000 Mexican migrants died trying to cross the border during the first decade of NAFTA. The annual number of deaths steadily increased during this time period, with almost 500 people dying in 2005, which constituted a doubling of the number of deaths that occurred the year prior to NAFTA being implemented.[29]

Ultimately, the structural violence that forcibly displaces Mexican peasants from their lands too often results in their deaths in the harsh desert border terrain they are forced to traverse in a desperate attempt to seek out a viable means of subsistence. In reference to the increasing numbers of migrant farmworkers in the United States, a Food First report points out, 'This dramatic migration of farmworkers, the vast majority from Mexico, can be traced to neoliberal, free-market reforms like NAFTA.'[30]

As Food First notes, it is not only Mexicans that are driven by structural violence to emigrate. Tens of thousands of economic refugees from Central American and Caribbean nations who have been dispossessed of their lands and livelihoods have also desperately sought to enter the United States illegally. According to the US Agency for International Development (USAID), 'The lack of economic opportunities in Latin America and the Caribbean makes the region the number one source of illegal immigration into the United States, with 88% of illegal immigrants coming from these countries.'[31] Ironically, the nation that is instrumental in causing their human suffering is also seen as their salvation.

For instance, the exodus of Salvadoreans fleeing the country's civil conflict during the 1980s did not end with the signing of peace accords in 1992. Salvadoreans have continued emigrating en masse, not to escape the physical violence of war, but rather to avoid the structural violence inherent in neoliberalism. Consequently, El Salvador's leading export under neoliberal globalization is not the textiles manufactured in the country's maquiladoras, but rather its people. By the early twenty-first century, it was estimated that 700 Salvadoreans were leaving the country each day in search of jobs, primarily in the United States. This process has torn apart families and communities that have become dependent on those members living in the United States who send money home. The 2.5 million Salvadoreans who live in the United States amount to more than one-third of the population of El Salvador. These economic refugees sent back $3.3 billion in remittances to family members in 2006, equivalent to 17 per cent of the country's GDP and more than the total of all foreign investment and development aid.[32] In essence, the economy in El Salvador would collapse if the flow of remittances from those who cannot support themselves in their home country under the neoliberal model were to cease. This phenomenon is also evident in other parts of the world as increasing numbers of economic refugees from Africa and Asia seek to escape the structural violence inherent in capitalism by illegally entering wealthy nations in Europe and North America as well as Australia.

The plight faced by dispossessed peasants in Mexico and other Latin American nations illustrates how the structural violence inherent in capitalism creates the conditions under which marginalized peoples become increasingly susceptible to direct physical violence. The process is evident in the dramatic rise in criminal and gang violence throughout the region. As Benedicte Bull notes,

> Criminal violence has reached epidemic levels in Latin America. Half of the ten countries with the highest homicide rate in the world are found in the region ... One expression of this wave of violence is the increased strength of gangs and transnational organised crime, which ... can no longer be viewed as isolated groups but instead reflect the emergence of a new social, criminal class.[33]

The wealthy in Latin America protect themselves from this violence by surrounding themselves with armed guards and bulletproof vehicles and by living in gated communities under a class-based apartheid system. Some even contribute to the violence by sponsoring 'social cleansing', which involves the killing of 'undesirables' such as drug addicts, the homeless, petty thieves, prostitutes and any other form of street dwellers. In many instances, local businesses and wealthy property owners hire death squads, usually consisting of off-duty police officers, to cleanse their neighbourhoods of these so-called undesirables.[34] In 2008 there were more than 3,000 murders – an average of 12 a day – in the city of Recife in Brazil, with many of the victims being street children, some as young as 10 years of age, who survived by begging, stealing and engaging in prostitution. One death squad member claimed that he was performing a 'social service' and that 'the price to have somebody killed would actually depend on the type of person you want killed'.[35] As one community organizer critical of the death squads explained, 'It's a perverse kind of killing. I call it social cleansing because the people being killed are normally black, they're poor and they're from the slums that surround the city. They have become what I call "the killables".'[36]

In Mexico, indeed throughout Latin America and much of the global South, displaced peasants forced into cities by structural violence have become particularly vulnerable to the physical violence related to criminal activities, thereby resulting in them becoming victims of the structural genocide being perpetrated by capital. Meanwhile, the structural genocide that results from millions of people in Mexico and throughout Latin America being dispossessed of their land and livelihood establishes the necessary conditions required by capital to continue on its never-ending quest to accumulate.

FARMER SUICIDES IN INDIA

The agricultural policies of the WTO, the IMF and the World Bank have negatively impacted farmers throughout the global South in much the same way as NAFTA has affected Mexican farmers. In 2003, when the representatives of the WTO met in Cancún, Mexico, to discuss international trade, more than 10,000 demonstrators amassed outside the meeting complex to protest against WTO agricultural policies. One of those protesters was a 55-year-old farmer named Lee Kyung Hae, who was part of a farmers' delegation from South Korea. In front of his fellow protesters and thousands of police officers, Lee stabbed himself to death. Lee's suicide was the ultimate act of protest against the WTO's agricultural policies. A colleague of Lee's explained, 'Korean farmers' lives are devastated by WTO policies. Their lives are getting worse. There is a huge amount of debt. Sometimes the farmers commit suicide at home. No one knew he was going to do this, but he did it to express his anger.'[37]

While Lee's sensational protest suicide received widespread media coverage, the plight of hundreds of thousands of other farmers in the global South who are killing themselves out of economic desperation is being ignored. Perhaps the starkest and most disturbing example of the structural violence perpetrated through the policies of the WTO and other international institutions is a suicide crisis among small farmers in India that is occurring on a genocidal scale. Between 1997 and 2009, according to the Indian government, some 216,500 Indian farmers committed suicide, which breaks down to more than 16,600 suicides a year – or one every thirty minutes.[38] The common denominator is that all of the farmers who have committed suicide were deep in debt. In fact, the number of Indian peasant households in debt doubled between 1991 and 2001 from 26 per cent to 48.6 per cent.[39]

When the WTO was established in the mid-1990s, the United States and the European Union responded to the interests of large agribusinesses by insisting that agricultural subsidies be permitted despite the fact that they contradicted free-trade doctrine. But while WTO rules permitting agricultural subsidies apply equally to all countries, the IMF and the World Bank have routinely required that nations in the global South unilaterally reduce their agricultural subsidies under the structural adjustment programs (SAPs) attached to their loans. Ultimately, then, the combination of policies promoted by the WTO, the IMF and the World Bank result in governments of wealthy nations in the global North being allowed to subsidize their agricultural corporations – in accordance with WTO regulations – while many countries in the global South are forced to eliminate so-called artificial trade barriers such as subsidies in order to adhere to conditions placed on loans issued by the IMF and the World Bank. It is precisely this combination of policies by international institutions serving the interests of capital that lies at the root of the structural genocide being perpetrated against farmers in India and other nations in the global South.

For thousands of years, farmers in the global South engaged in traditional farming practices that focused primarily on cultivating food crops for subsistence and for local markets, thereby ensuring a degree of food security. A core component of this practice was the concept of seed saving. After every crop harvest, farmers would save seeds to plant the following year. In other words, the seeds were free; they were part of the commons. However, according to Vandana Shiva,

This seed freedom is a major obstacle for seed corporations. To create a market for seed the seed has to be transformed materially so that its reproductive ability is blocked. Its legal status must also be changed so that instead of being the common property of farming communities, it becomes the patented private property of the seed corporations.[40]

The intellectual property rights provisions negotiated during the Uruguay Round (1986–94) of talks under the General Agreement on Tariffs and Trade (GATT) sought to overcome this 'obstacle' by establishing rules pertaining to patents and copyrights. According to Milton Friedman, 'In both patents and copyrights, there is clearly a strong *prima facie* case for establishing property rights. Unless this is done, the inventor will find it difficult or impossible to collect a payment for the contribution his invention makes to output. He will, that is, confer benefits on others for which he cannot be compensated.'[41] GATT sought to link the intellectual property rights referred to by Friedman to seeds and to international trade, thereby ensuring that large agribusinesses could obtain patents for genetically modified (GM) and hybrid seeds in order to 'collect a payment for the contribution' they provided to the 'output' of small farmers around the world.

But corporations do not 'invent' the GM and hybrid seeds; they simply modify existing seeds. Furthermore, the research that leads to these so-called inventions is based on the results of centuries of seed breeding by peasant farmers whose knowledge has been passed down over generations and has traditionally been considered a 'commons'. The intellectual property rights regime allows agribusinesses to patent GM and hybrid seeds to sell for profit while peasants receive no financial remuneration for generations of intellectual input into the process. In short, corporations are engaged in what has been called bio-piracy. According to philosopher Michael Hardt, bio-piracy consists of

the processes whereby transnational corporations expropriate the common in the form of indigenous knowledges or genetic information from plants, animals and humans, usually through the use of patents. Traditional knowledges concerning, for instance, the use of a ground seed as a natural pesticide, or the healing qualities of a particular plant, are turned into private property by the corporation that patents the knowledge. Parenthetically I would insist that piracy is a misnomer for such activities. Pirates have a much more noble vocation: they steal property. These corporations instead steal the common and transform it into property.[42]

On 29 December 1992, in the midst of the GATT talks to establish the intellectual property rights regime, some 500 small farmers in India struck out against this new process of accumulation by dispossession by ransacking and destroying a factory in Bangalore owned by US-based Cargill's seed subsidiary. As philosopher Deane Curtin noted,

> Although their principal target was Cargill, the protest in a larger sense was against the intellectual property rights provisions of the GATT.... In another carefully chosen symbol, after U.S. trade representative Carla Hills had recently called on India's elite to 'pry open new markets with a crowbar,' the farmers chose crowbars as the instrument of choice for ransacking the factory.[43]

Despite such protests, the GATT was nevertheless transformed into the World Trade Organization (WTO) in 1995 and the Agreement on Trade-Related Intellectual Property Rights (TRIPS) was implemented. Thus India's agricultural sector was opened up to sterile GM and hybrid seeds patented by corporations such as Cargill, Monsanto and Syngenta that had to be purchased anew each year. These large agribusinesses began organizing workshops in India and other countries in the global South to teach small farmers how to industrialize their operations, cultivate crops for export and increase their yield. Consequently, many farmers began taking out loans to cover the costs of seeds and other inputs in order to produce cash crops for the global market. Armed with their new knowledge, inputs and the promise of higher incomes, millions of farmers shifted from traditional agricultural practices that had served them so well for generations to cultivating crops for export. According to the promoters of this neoliberal export model – governments, international institutions and agribusinesses – the annual purchase of seeds and other necessary inputs such as fertilizers and pesticides would not constitute a financial burden because farmers would earn higher revenues from increased yields.

But the promised increases in yields and income did not materialize. In India, farmers were told that biotech cotton seeds would yield 1,500 kilograms of cotton per acre. Most farmers, however, only achieved an average annual yield of 200 kilograms. Instead of enjoying projected income increases of 10,000 rupees per acre, many farmers were losing 6,000 rupees per acre.[44] Farmers were then forced to borrow more money to cover their losses and to purchase new seeds in order to plant the following year's crop, thus initiating a downward spiral that has led them deeper into debt every year.

Returning to subsistence farming is not an option because once farmers become indebted to banks or unscrupulous moneylenders they have little choice but to continue cultivating cash crops in the hope of generating the necessary income required to make their loan payments. As Shiva notes, 'A peasant switching to hybrid or genetically modified (GM) seeds finds him or herself, in a year's time, two to three hundred thousand rupees in debt. ... It's seed freedom for the corporations but seed slavery for the peasants.'[45]

It is not only the failure to achieve promised yield levels that has hurt Indian farmers and contributed to their indebtedness, but also the WTO-permitted subsidies provided by the US government to US agribusinesses. The US Farm Act of 2002 increased the already high levels of subsidies by $82 billion a year. Agribusinesses in the cotton sector enjoyed a $4 billion increase in annual subsidies, which contributed to a doubling of US cotton exports and a flooding of the global market.[46] Consequently, the livelihoods of Indian and African cotton farmers have been devastated because, with only minimal or no subsidies of their own, their costs of production often surpass cotton's market value. This process led Palagummi Sainath to ask and answer the question,

What does the WTO do in this situation? It tells the poor countries to diversify their products. In other words, the US will not lower its subsidies, the EU will not lower its subsidies; you grow something else! The demand of being market-friendly and viable is one made of the poorest farmers on earth, not of the richest.[47]

Some 70 per cent of India's population of 1.2 billion live in rural regions and the overwhelming majority still depend on agriculture for their livelihood. In 2009, an estimated 50 per cent of the rural population lived in poverty, with that figure surpassing 80 per cent in the country's poorest states.[48] The neoliberal policies that have left Indian farmers indebted and impoverished have contributed to the process of urbanization as tens of thousands of farmers and their families have abandoned their lands and migrated to the slums in India's cities in search of jobs.

The neoliberal restructuring of India's economy during the 1990s led to a hi-tech boom in a handful of cities and to soaring stock market indexes. This process resulted in the creation of 1 million new millionaires in the country and a growing middle class that has been held up as a shining example of neoliberal development. However, there has been little focus on the fact that the number of Indians living in poverty increased by 56 million during these 'boom' years.[49] Due to a lack of education and job skills, many migrants to the cities fail to gain access to hi-tech jobs and end up instead working in the informal sector or as low-wage labourers. Consequently, the urbanization process is not alleviating the economic hardships faced by farmers who migrate to the cities because for many peasants rural poverty is simply being replaced with urban poverty. As Sainath sarcastically points out, 'In the last 15 years, the fastest growing sector in this country is not IT; it's not software, its inequality. It has grown faster than at anytime in our history.'[50]

With few opportunities in the cities and faced with a never-ending spiral of indebtedness in the countryside, many farmers simply reach the point of despair that leads them to take their own lives. In 2009, more than 17,000 farmers committed suicide, often by drinking the pesticides that they had purchased from the corporations who sold them the seeds.[51] Shiva directly linked the suicide epidemic to the introduction of GM seeds:

> The highest rates of suicide are in Andhra Pradesh and Punjab, two states with the highest dependence on cash crops, the highest penetration of Monsanto's seeds, and the highest levels of corporatized agriculture. The states in which farmers are using their own seeds and growing crops for their sustenance and local markets are avoiding the debt trap that forces farmers into despair and hopelessness.[52]

Monsanto has claimed that its biotech cotton seeds are not responsible for farmer suicides, placing the blame instead on indebtedness. According to the company, 'Farmer suicide has numerous causes with most experts agreeing that indebtedness is one of the main factors. Farmers unable to repay loans and facing spiralling interest often see suicide as the only solution.'[53] But the company's attempt to separate the purchase of its cotton seeds by Indian farmers from the debt problem faced by those same farmers constitutes a refusal to acknowledge the structural violence inherent in capitalism. After all, the indebtedness endured by Indian farmers is directly related to the intellectual property rights accorded to corporations such as Monsanto in order to boost capital accumulation by forcing farmers to borrow money in order to purchase patented seeds.

Disturbingly, the tragic phenomenon of farmer suicides appears to be on the rise in other regions of the global South. For instance, as many as 2,000 farmers in Kenya took their own lives in 2010 after massive crop failures left them unable to pay their debts. Shifting rainfall patterns and prolonged droughts related to climate change led to a massive failure of corn crops in eastern Kenya. Since 2008, many farmers have used their farms as collateral for loans in order to obtain sufficient funding to purchase patented seeds. But according to agricultural economist Stanley Karuga, many of the seeds developed by corporations are inappropriate for the changing climate conditions. Consequently, unable to feed themselves and their families, and faced with having their farms repossessed, many farmers have turned to suicide.[54]

International trade and intellectual property rights agreements that prioritize capital's inherent need to accumulate constitute structural violence perpetrated against hundreds of thousands of farmers in India and other regions of the global South. And, as Shiva notes, 'The groups perpetrating the violence include the WTO, the World Bank and the IMF, global agribusiness corporations, and governments.'[55] In other words, the entities that established the structures responsible for the structural genocide are those responsible for serving the interests of capital.

CONCLUSION

While the free market generally provides capital with the freedom that permits it to expand and accumulate, capital is not ideologically bound to the doctrine, as the cases of Mexico and India make evident. Therefore the structures, institutions and policies at the heart of neoliberal globalization do not always adhere to the free-market doctrine; rather, they abide by the logic of capital in that they enhance capital's ability to expand and accumulate. Consequently, there is no contradiction in neoliberalism; it is doing precisely what it is intended to do – serve the interests of capital. Therefore it is perfectly rational for international institutions to implement seemingly contradictory policies such as those that permit governments in the global North to provide agricultural subsidies to large agribusinesses while prohibiting governments in the global South from doing the same.

Capital is content to violate the most basic tenets of the free-market doctrine if doing so increases its capacity to expand and accumulate. When viewed in this light, subsidies for agribusinesses and government bailouts of the banking sector are perfectly rational interventions under the logic of capital. As Jim Stanford noted earlier, governments will always intervene; the questions are how and in whose interests. And, as neoliberalism

makes evident, the interventions of liberal democratic governments are primarily dictated by the logic of capital.

When capital dispossesses peasants of their knowledge, lands
and livelihoods, it places them at greater risk of death from
direct physical violence – either at their own hands or at the
hands of others – as the cases of Mexico and India make evident.
In this manner, structural violence is an accomplice to physical
violence in Mexico, India and other nations of the global South
where the deaths of hundreds of thousands of people constitute
structural genocide.

4

STRUCTURAL GENOCIDE:
THE CASE OF SUB-SAHARAN AFRICA

Why is it that a child's death amounts to a tragedy, but the death
of millions is merely a statistic?

Patrick McDonald

The region of the world that has been most severely impacted
by capitalism's structural genocide is sub-Saharan Africa. The
region has a sordid history of brutality under European colonialism, with perhaps the starkest example of accumulation by
dispossession being the shipping of some 12 million Africans to
the Americas to work as slaves in the service of capital – with
1.5 million of them dying in transit.[1] Capitalism's structural
genocide has continued to target Africans disproportionately
to this day.

More than half a million women die globally each year as a
result of complications of pregnancy and childbirth, and 99 per
cent of these deaths occur in the global South – most of them
in sub-Saharan Africa. As one United Nations report explains,
'Almost all of these deaths could be prevented if women in developing countries had access to adequate diets, safe water and
sanitation facilities, basic literacy and health services during
pregnancy and childbirth.'[2] Additionally, according to the World

Health Organization, 2 million people worldwide died of AIDS in 2008, with a disproportionate number – 1.4 million – of the deaths occurring in sub-Saharan Africa. In total, the AIDS epidemic has orphaned more than 14 million children in the region. Even more troubling is the fact that the scale of this humanitarian catastrophe is not likely to diminish significantly in the near future given that more than half of the 6.7 million people in sub-Saharan Africa infected with HIV/AIDS still lack access to life-saving antiretroviral drugs.[3]

Meanwhile, in 2008, according to a study commissioned by the WHO and UNICEF, 6 million children globally died before reaching their fifth birthday due to preventable or treatable diseases such as diarrhoea, pneumonia and malaria. Many of these diseases resulted from immune deficiencies caused by hunger and malnutrition. Almost half of these child deaths occurred in sub-Saharan Africa.[4] The common denominator in the overwhelming majority of all of the aforementioned preventable deaths is global inequality – in both power and wealth. As Michael Brie noted in 2009,

> In the past six years more children have died globally as a result of starvation and preventable diseases than humans perished in the six years of the Second World War. Every three seconds a human life that just began ceases to exist in a cruel way. At the same time in these same three seconds $120,000 are being spent on military armaments world wide.[5]

The cause of the immense suffering resulting from hunger cannot simply be reduced to a global food shortage or overpopulation; it rests in the unequal distribution of the global food supply, which is a direct result of neoliberal policies. Under neoliberal globalization, African nations have been forced to follow the path of most other countries in the global South by prioritizing the cultivation of crops for export over production for domestic consumption. The result has been massive food insecurity and widespread hunger. At the height of decolonization in the mid-1960s, Africa was a net exporter of food. But Africa now imports 25 per cent of its food, with virtually every nation being a net importer.[6] One of the reasons for this dramatic shift is the conditions placed on IMF and World Bank loans that require countries to produce non-food crops for export in order to generate sufficient foreign reserves to service their debts. In 1986, US agriculture secretary John Block claimed 'the idea that developing countries should feed themselves is an anachronism from a bygone era. They could better ensure their food security by relying on U.S. agricultural products, which are available, in most cases at lower cost.'[7] Block failed to mention that US agricultural products were only cheaper because of massive government subsidies provided to agribusinesses. Meanwhile, conditions placed on IMF and World Bank loans prevented African governments from providing similar subsidies to their own agricultural sectors.

In many countries, the best agricultural land soon became dominated by non-food crops cultivated for export while food crops for domestic consumption were increasingly displaced to regions with poor soil conditions. And when global prices for export crops such as cocoa and coffee plummeted due to overproduction – resulting from too many farmers throughout the global South being pushed to produce the same crops – many peasants in Africa found that the income they were earning from their export crops proved insufficient to purchase the imported foodstuffs promoted by Block. Ultimately, according to Walden Bello, the 'policies promoted by the World Bank, IMF, and WTO systematically discouraged food self-sufficiency and encouraged food importation by destroying the local productive base of smallholder agriculture.'[8]

This situation has been further exacerbated by the fact that relatively wealthy nations such as Saudi Arabia and South Korea recently began buying or leasing farmland in more than a dozen sub-Saharan African nations to grow crops to feed their own populations. In recent years, Saudi investors have invested extensively in land in Sudan, Ethiopia and Kenya to cultivate wheat to feed the Saudi population. Meanwhile, China has leased 2.8

million hectares of land in the Democratic Republic of the Congo to grow palm oil to produce agrofuels, also known as biofuels. Similarly, European investors have recently acquired 3.9 million hectares of land in Africa to cultivate crops to produce agrofuels for use in Europe. In some of these countries, the land-grab is increasing food insecurity by exacerbating already-existing food shortages.[9]

The profit motive driving capitalism is in direct conflict with basic human need with regard to food, one of the fundamental necessities required for human survival. Capitalist logic requires that food be distributed to those who can afford not only to purchase what they require in order to subsist, but to purchase as much as their gluttonous appetites desire. Consequently, many in the United States and other wealthy nations enjoy an abundance of choice in their diet while millions of people in sub-Saharan Africa go hungry because they do not constitute a viable market according to the logic of capital.[10]

Agricultural policies that serve the interests of capital consti-tute structural violence that results in almost 3 million children in sub-Saharan Africa dying annually from hunger-related diseases. Capital's response to this crisis is to deliver food aid through mechanisms that further enhance its ability to accumulate. The United States provides more than $1 billion in food aid to Africa annually, but only one-tenth of that amount in long-term development aid.[11] The consequence is the continued dependence of millions of Africans on food aid provided by wealthy nations rather than achieving food security. Furthermore, under US law, the government's food aid money must purchase food from US agricultural producers and at least 75 per cent of that food must be shipped to Africa by US-registered shipping companies.[12] As a result, almost half of the aid money goes to cover shipping costs, thereby diminishing dramatically the amount of food that reaches hungry Africans.

US food aid regulations are more focused on finding markets for surplus US agricultural commodities and advancing US geo-political interests than aiding people in need. If providing food to hungry people was the priority, then purchasing food from African countries that have surplus crops would result in much lower transportation costs and allow twice as much food to reach those in need while simultaneously contributing to food security in the region. In 2005, a proposal to change US laws governing food aid to allow for food to be purchased in the region where it is needed was defeated due to the lobbying efforts of the agribusiness sector and shipping companies.[13]

Multinational agribusinesses are also using US food aid programmes to promote their patented GM crops as the solution to world hunger rather than the return of Africa's agricultural land to smallholders to cultivate food crops for domestic consumption. The US government has responded to those African nations that have resisted the GM food by threatening to cut off all food aid.[14] Ultimately, US food aid to Africa constitutes a massive corporate welfare programme that facilitates capital accumulation for US agribusinesses and shipping companies while, in conjunction with neoliberal policies, undermining food security for millions of Africans.

THE BUSINESS OF HEALTH CARE

For people in sub-Saharan Africa, structural violence hits them with a one-two punch. First, agriculture policies that favour capital constitute structural violence that causes hunger and malnutrition. Second, the logic of capital that drives pharmaceuticals companies to maximize profits prevents Africans from accessing life-saving medicines for those diseases that often result from hunger and malnutrition. The result is structural genocide.

The principal barrier to addressing the deaths of millions of people annually from preventable and treatable diseases is the logic of capital, with its inherent need to accumulate wealth through the maximization of profits. As Martin L. Hirsch points out, 'Corporate governance in pharmaceutical companies that focuses on the shareholder's bottom line is completely inconsistent with health care, medicine and access to pharmaceuticals, where the patient should come first.'[15] In other words, pharmaceuticals companies adhere to the logic of capital by focusing on the research and development of those drugs that generate the greatest profit rather than ensuring that the basic health-care needs of everyone are met. Consequently, as Hirsch explains,

> Pharmaceutical companies have been accused of keeping lifesaving treatment beyond the reach of the world's poor. ... Drug companies are criticized for focusing their research on such matters as baldness, toe fungus, and erectile dysfunction rather than global epidemics, especially those plaguing poor countries. Rather than focus on curing life threatening diseases, global pharmaceutical companies research and produce what are called lifestyle drugs, because there is far more money to be made selling these types of drugs. Lifestyle drugs are sold for large profits, whereas drugs to treat the poor amount to a losing endeavor because the people who need the drugs cannot afford to pay the high prices the pharmaceuticals companies charge in order to maximize profits.[16]

Not surprisingly, 'lifestyle' drugs, which address non-life-threatening conditions such as baldness, wrinkles, acne and impotence, are predominantly targeted towards consumers in the global North who have sufficient disposable income to indulge themselves in these commodities. It is a perfectly 'rational' business decision under the logic of capital for pharmaceuticals companies to produce 'lifestyle' drugs for relatively wealthy people in North America and Europe instead of medicines that would prevent the deaths of millions of poor people in sub-Saharan Africa. And this 'rational' business decision is a prime example of the internal logic of a social system that prioritizes production for profit over production for human need. Furthermore, such rational business decisions require that both the decision-makers in the pharmaceuticals companies and consumers in the global North exist in a state of denial, or 'wilful blindness', regarding the fact that their choices constitute a form of structural genocide against millions of people in the global South, particularly in sub-Saharan Africa.

This discrepancy is not limited to 'lifestyle' drugs; it is also evident in the research-and-development decisions of the world's largest pharmaceuticals companies with regard to life-threatening diseases. Communicable diseases such as malaria, tuberculosis and AIDS, as well as diarrhoea caused by communicable diseases, are the leading cause of death from illness in sub-Saharan Africa, whereas non-communicable diseases like cancer and heart disease are the leading killers in wealthy nations in the global North. In 2008, according to a WHO report, there were 665 drugs being actively developed by the world's ten largest pharmaceuticals companies, but only 74 – 11 per cent – of them were for communicable diseases.[17] Of the $43 billion spent by companies on research and development that year to address communicable and non-communicable diseases, almost $30 billion of it, or 68 per cent, went to developing drugs for the latter. There was a similar distribution pattern in the disbursement of public funding for drug research and development in the five wealthy nations – the United States, United Kingdom, France, Germany and Japan – examined in the WHO report. In total, more money is spent on researching and developing drugs to address just two non-communicable diseases – cancer and heart disease – prevalent in the wealthy nations of the global North than for all communicable diseases combined.[18]

As a result of these rational business decisions, many of the drugs that do exist to address communicable diseases in the global South are obsolete and in dire need of updating. As Hirsch notes,

> Of the forty-one important drugs used to treat tropical diseases, diseases primarily affecting developing countries, none were discovered in the 1990s and all but six were discovered before 1985. Sleeping sickness, a disease that affects 300,000 Africans each year, can only be treated with the same drug that was used to treat it seventy years ago. The last drug company that made a more effective treatment discontinued the product because it was not profitable.[19]

The disproportionate financial investments made by pharmaceuticals companies in 'lifestyle' drugs and medicines for non-communicable diseases are not restricted to the costs of research and development; nor do they even constitute the principal expense of these corporations. Pharmaceuticals companies often spend more on marketing their drug products than on developing and producing them. In 2004, for example, pharmaceuticals companies in the United States invested $31.5 billion in research and development, but spent almost double that amount – $57.5 billion – on marketing their products, primarily to consumers in the global North.[20]

While the plight of the poor in sub-Saharan Africa is often neglected with regard to the development of drugs to address the most life-threatening illnesses that impact them, those same people are often eagerly sought out by pharmaceuticals companies to serve as guinea pigs in clinical trials of new experimental drugs. In one case of drug testing by the multinational pharmaceuticals giant Pfizer, the company sought to conduct clinical trials for a new experimental drug for meningitis called Trovan, which was forecast to earn the company up to $1 billion annually in revenues. Pfizer had yet to receive US Federal Drug Administration (FDA) approval for the drug when a meningitis epidemic broke out in Nigeria in 1996. Pfizer quickly dispatched researchers to the country to conduct clinical trials of Trovan on nearly a hundred children and infants. Five of the children who were given Trovan in the clinical trials conducted in the state of Kano died. The company kept the deaths a secret, and the following year, unaware of the tragedy in Nigeria, the FDA deemed Trovan to be safe for adults. But then, in 1999, the FDA severely restricted use of the drug due to reports of liver damage and death. Meanwhile, European regulators banned the drug entirely.[21]

The deaths of the Nigerian children did not become public knowledge until the *Washington Post* published an investigation into overseas pharmaceuticals testing in 2000. The Nigerian government responded to the article by launching an investigation headed by a team of medical experts, who later released a report condemning Pfizer's clinical testing as 'an illegal trial of an unregistered drug' and a 'clear case of exploitation of the ignorant'.[22] Congressman Tom Lantos of California, the senior Democrat on the International Relations Committee, responded to the report by stating, 'I think it borders on the criminal that the large pharmaceutical companies, both here and in Europe, are using these poor, illiterate and uninformed people as guinea pigs.'[23] Meanwhile, Pfizer claims that it obtained verbal permission from the parents of the children. However, the company failed to obtain permission from the Nigerian government to conduct the testing. It also violated FDA regulations on overseas testing by not obtaining approval from an ethics committee.[24]

In 2009, Pfizer settled one of the several lawsuits it is facing in relation to the illegal clinical trials by agreeing to pay $75 million to the Kano state government as compensation for the deaths of the children. Other cases brought against the company by the Nigerian national government and survivors of the trials are still pending.[25] Naturally, such criminal and civil charges, and the related payouts, are neither good for business nor good for Pfizer's stock value. A classified cable disclosed by Wikileaks that the US embassy in the Nigerian capital of Abuja sent to the US State Department in April 2009 illustrates the lengths to which corporations are willing to go in order to address such public relations problems. In reference to a meeting between Pfizer's country manager Enrico Liggeri and embassy officials, the classified cable stated:

> According to Liggeri, Pfizer had hired investigators to uncover corruption links to federal attorney general Michael Aondoakaa to expose him and put pressure on him to drop the federal cases. He said Pfizer's investigators were passing this information to local media ... A series of damaging articles detailing Aondoakaa's 'alleged' corruption ties were published in February and March. Liggeri contended that Pfizer had much more damaging information on Aondoakaa and that Aondoakaa's cronies were pressuring him to drop the suit for fear of further negative articles.[26]

At no point did Pfizer admit any wrongdoing or engage in any form of humanitarian response by voluntarily offering some form of reparation to the families of the victims. Instead, the company's resources were used to pressure the Nigerian government into dropping the lawsuit.

Even when pharmaceuticals companies and governments of wealthy nations obtain permission from national governments to conduct clinical tests in sub-Saharan Africa, there is little protection for participants. For a variety of reasons, including pressure from the US government and pharmaceuticals companies, or simply a desire to help their dying citizens, governments ensure that companies can conduct experiments free from regulatory interference. Benjamin Mason Meier notes that 'African nations have shown great reluctance to impose any restrictions on human research, thereby creating a medical "race to the bottom" at the expense of human rights and human life.'[27]

It is not only multinational pharmaceuticals companies that exploit the lack of regulations in many African nations, but also the US government. In 1994, the Centers for Disease Control (CDC) and the National Institutes of Health (NIH) began testing the HIV/AIDS drug Zidoduvine (AZT) on 17,000 pregnant African women infected with HIV/AIDS in order to determine the amount of AZT required to prevent the disease from being passed on to an unborn child. But, as Meier states,

> Although U.S. government agencies were conducting the testing, these experiments took place without regard for U.S. medical research standards ... Some U.S. scientific experts quickly denounced the testing as unethical. ... In addition to conflicting with U.S. law, the AZT experiments took place in violation of international ethical standards.[28]

The testing practices of the pharmaceuticals industry illustrate how, within the structures of global capitalism, poor Africans do not enjoy the same degree of human rights as most citizens of wealthy nations in the global North. It is not surprising that impoverished Africans with terminal illnesses, who lack access to adequate health care, would be willing to act as human guinea pigs in ways that would be unacceptable to most in the global

North. Perhaps the greatest travesty is the fact that many of the impoverished Africans used in this drug testing cannot afford to purchase those same drugs once they go on the market.

THE AIDS EPIDEMIC

When HIV/AIDS reached epidemic proportions in sub-Saharan Africa during the 1990s, the majority of those suffering from the virus could not access the same drugs that were saving the lives of millions of people in North America and Europe. The prices that pharmaceuticals companies charged for the life-saving drugs were simply too high for poor Africans. As a 2001 article published in *Time* magazine explained,

> Despite years of evidence of AIDS' genocidal toll on poor countries, no one has brought these drugs within reach of ordinary Africans. In fact, the people who make the drugs – American- and European-owned multinational pharmaceutical corporations – and their home governments, notably Washington, have worked hard to keep prices up by limiting exports to the Third World and vigorously enforcing patent rights.[29]

According to the United Nations Development Programme (UNDP), the AIDS epidemic has single-handedly reduced life expectancy in sub-Saharan Africa by twenty years, down to 46 years of age for most people in the region – thirty-two years lower than the average for people in the global North.[30] As much as 30 per cent of the population of some sub-Saharan African countries are infected with HIV/AIDS.[31] The social and economic costs of the AIDS epidemic have proven devastating in many countries in sub-Saharan Africa. According to Joia S. Mukherjee,

> In Zambia, two-thirds of families who lose the head of the household experience an 80 per cent drop in monthly income. In the Ivory Coast, families who lose an adult to HIV experience a 50 per cent decrease in household income. Agricultural productivity in Burkina Faso has fallen by 20 per cent because of AIDS. In Ethiopia, HIV-positive farmers spend between 11.6 and 16.4 hours a week farming compared with 33.6 hours weekly for healthy farmers....

In Swaziland, school enrolment fell by 36 per cent, mainly because girls left school to care for sick relatives.[32]

By the time that HIV/AIDS had reached epidemic proportions in the mid-1990s, most governments in sub-Saharan Africa did not have the money required to address the crisis effectively, in part because much of their revenue was needed to service their large foreign debts. The structural adjustment programs imposed on these nations by international lending institutions often required the slashing of spending on social services such as health care and education in order to make money available to service their debts. As Nana K. Poku pointed out in 2002,

> at a time when up to 70 per cent of adults in some hospitals are suffering from AIDS-related illnesses – placing extreme pressure on health services – many African countries have had to cut their health expenditure in order to satisfy IMF and World Bank conditionalities. Such circumstances make it almost impossible to treat those with the virus effectively, or to undertake effective campaigns to reduce high-risk behaviour and provide essential resources in the fight against the pandemic. For example ... the Tanzanian government spends in excess of three times more on debt servicing each year than it does on health care.[33]

Nevertheless, national governments in the global South sought ways to address the AIDS crisis. Among the most radical options in the context of global capitalism were efforts to challenge the pharmaceuticals companies by producing or importing generic versions of patented AIDS drugs in order to make them more affordable. Under the WTO's TRIPS agreement, governments can issue 'compulsory licensing' that allows the manufacture of generic versions of patented drugs for domestic use, but only in cases of national emergency. As a result, the generic version of a patented antiretroviral drug combination cocktail for AIDS that costs between $10,000 and $15,000 in the United States sells for only $3,000 in Brazil and $1,000 in India.[34] While these measures promised to save millions of lives, the pharmaceuticals companies and the US government were not about to tolerate the threat that they posed to the interests of capital.

During the 1990s, deaths from AIDS in the United States declined significantly, in large part because most of those infected
with the disease had access to life-saving drugs. During the
same period, deaths in sub-Saharan Africa and other parts of
the global South skyrocketed. South Africa was the nation with
the most people living with AIDS; while there were a number
of factors (i.e. culture) that influenced the levels of prevalence,
the principal obstacle to providing treatment was the cost of
drugs. At that time, the antiretroviral drugs cost approximately
$12,000 a year in a nation in which the average annual income
was $2,600.[35]

In 1997, the South African government, after initially ignor-
ing the AIDS crisis, decided to address the problem by author-
izing the importation of cheaper generic versions of AIDS drugs
from India, which was not obligated to abide by the relevant
international patent rules until 2005. Pharmaceuticals companies immediately demanded that the policy be rescinded, claiming that the exporting and importing of generics violated the
TRIPS agreement of the WTO. The US government responded
on behalf of the multinational pharmaceuticals companies by
putting pressure on South Africa during bilateral trade talks
to reverse its decision on the generic drugs. And then, in 1998,
the US Congress conditioned development assistance to South
Africa on the US State Department having taken sufficient
steps to pressure South Africa to reverse its generic drugs
policy.[36] Vice President Al Gore was at the forefront of the US
government's efforts to force South Africa to acquiesce to the
demands of the pharmaceuticals companies, leading consumer
activist and presidential candidate Ralph Nader to chastise
him for engaging in 'an astonishing array of bullying tactics to
prevent South Africa from implementing policies, legal under
international trade rules, that are designed to expand access
to HIV/AIDS drugs'.[37] In the meantime, thirty-nine pharmaceuticals companies filed a lawsuit against the South African
government claiming that the 1997 law violated their patent
rights.

In January 2001, the US government opened a second front in its war to defend the interests of capital when it filed charges in the WTO against Brazil on behalf of US-based pharmaceuticals companies, claiming that the South American nation's 1996 Industrial Property Law violated the TRIPS agreement. The law required foreign companies to manufacture their patented products in Brazil within three years; otherwise compulsory licenses could be issued to produce generic versions of their products.

Brazil had the largest number of HIV/AIDS cases in Latin America and a 1996 law required that the government provide free antiretroviral drugs to everyone with the disease. The cost of purchasing patented drugs proved prohibitive and so the Brazilian government began licensing the domestic production of generic AIDS drugs under its Industrial Property Law, which led the US government to file its WTO complaint.[38] By 2002, the Brazilian national health system was providing free antiretroviral drugs to some 120,000 people with HIV/AIDS – up from zero in 1996 – which constituted virtually everyone in the country suffering from the disease.[39] Brazil's programme to combat HIV/AIDS became the most successful in the global South, almost halving the number of deaths from AIDS in the programme's first five years and achieving a prevalence rate of 0.6 per cent – equal to that in the United States.[40]

A massive global campaign conducted by more than one hundred NGOs defended the right of South Africa and Brazil to implement policies that saved the lives of their citizens. The campaign portrayed the United States and the pharmaceuticals companies as prioritizing profits over people's lives. Ultimately, the success of the Brazilian AIDS programme illustrated the inhumanity present in the positions held by the US government and the pharmaceuticals companies.

In response to the overwhelming political pressure resulting from the international campaign, the United States dropped its WTO complaint against Brazil in June 2001. The same year, the pharmaceuticals companies reached an agreement with the South

African government and dropped their lawsuit. The agreement required that South Africa purchase patented AIDS drugs from pharmaceuticals companies, but the drugs would be provided at significant discounts. For instance, pharmaceuticals giant Merck began supplying one of its AIDS drugs to South Africans for $600 a year.[41]

Many activists viewed the capitulation of the US government and the pharmaceuticals corporations as victories for social justice, but the companies were not giving up the fight. The companies had simply realized that if they failed to provide discounted drugs then countries would follow the examples set by South Africa and Brazil and issue compulsory licences for the domestic production, or the importation, of cheaper generics. The companies responded to this threat to their market share and their ability to maximize profits by negotiating discounts only where they did not believe they could successfully prevent compulsory licensing. In essence, the South African case had established a precedent in which individual governments in sub-Saharan Africa could negotiate discounts for the patented AIDS drugs produced by the multinational pharmaceuticals companies. However, the fact that South Africa's economy is the largest in the region gave its government a degree of leverage in its fight with the pharmaceuticals companies that others did not possess. Smaller and poorer nations quickly discovered that the pharmaceuticals companies were not about to offer the same rate of discount to them. In Senegal, for example, the price for patented AIDS drugs only dropped to $1,200 a year, which remained far too expensive in a country where the average annual income was $510.[42]

Further evidence that pharmaceuticals companies remain intent on challenging any threat to their ability to maximize profits is their continued reactions to Brazil's AIDS programme. In 2007 Brazil announced it was issuing a compulsory licence for the production of a generic version of Merck's patented AIDS drug Stocrin. Merck responded to Brazil's announcement by issuing a statement that declared:

This expropriation of intellectual property sends a chilling signal to research-based companies about the attractiveness of undertaking risky research on diseases that affect the developing world, potentially hurting patients who may require new and innovative life-saving therapies. Research and development-based pharmaceutical companies like Merck simply cannot sustain a situation in which the developed countries alone are expected to bear the cost for essential drugs in both least-developed countries and emerging markets.[43]

Merck's claim that pharmaceuticals companies cannot bear the costs for the development and provision of affordable drugs to address the AIDS epidemic in the global South does not add up when industry profits are analysed. The eight largest pharmaceuticals companies in the United States earned $61.7 billion in profits in 2009.[44] The numbers make apparent that the discounted AIDS drugs that companies such as Merck have so begrudgingly provided to nations in sub-Saharan Africa have not prevented them from earning massive profits. Furthermore, based on estimates by the United Nations, $7 billion in funding for AIDS drugs for 2010 would have provided life-saving medicines to the 3.8 million people in sub-Saharan Africa who were not receiving them and, in conjunction with government and NGO funding for prevention strategies, would have saved 1.3 million lives.[45] In other words, if the eight largest pharmaceuticals companies in the United States, whose profits for 2009 averaged $7.7 billion each, had each been willing to accept an average profit of $6.8 billion instead, the difference could have helped prevent 1.3 million AIDS deaths. Merck's $12.9 billion in profit alone for 2009 was almost double the amount of funding required the following year to address adequately the AIDS crisis in sub-Saharan Africa.[46]

As for the US government, which so eagerly defended the ability of pharmaceuticals companies to maximize profits at the expense of human lives, it spent $700 billion on its military in 2010.[47] A minuscule 1 per cent reduction in US military spending would have made sufficient funding available to provide

life-saving drugs to every AIDS-infected person in sub-Saharan
Africa who lacked access to them.

The failure to implement such a seemingly rational solution
to the AIDS crisis illustrates the power of the internal logic of
capital, to which pharmaceuticals companies are compelled to
adhere in order to maximize profits. Ironically, given that these
companies are supposedly in the health business, this logic does
not allow them to prioritize human well-being. And as for the
possibility of regulating these companies so that they will place
human need before profit, the US government's support of the
pharmaceuticals industry illustrates the degree to which the state
in a liberal democracy prioritizes the interests of capital.

Despite more than fifteen years of struggle to ensure that
everyone in the global South can receive life-saving AIDS drugs,
millions have died unnecessarily, and more than 5 million people
with the virus still lack access to essential medicines. There is
no clearer illustration of the shortcomings in trying to reform
the behaviour of capital than the ongoing annihilation of poor
people in sub-Saharan Africa who are dying as a direct result
of the structural violence inherent in capitalism. As Joia S.
Mukherjee notes, 'Structural violence, defined as the physical
and psychological harm that results from exploitive and unjust
social, political and economic systems, is the shadow in which
the AIDS virus lurks.'[48]

THE MILLENNIUM DEVELOPMENT GOALS

The Millennium Development Goals established in 2000 were
intended to address the most pressing social concerns for impoverished people in the global South. Among the goals is the
halving of poverty and hunger by 2015, as compared to 1990
levels; the reduction of child mortality by two-thirds; and the
achievement of full and productive employment for all. Even if
the project is successful, millions of people in the global South
will continue to suffer from hunger and poverty in 2015 and 2
million children each year will still die before they reach the

age of 5. And yet, even given these relatively modest objectives, the United Nations reported: 'At the midway point between their adoption in 2000 and the 2015 target date for achieving the Millennium Development Goals, sub-Saharan Africa is not on track to achieve any of the Goals.'[49]

One fundamental problem with the Millennium Development Goals is that their success is predicated on the very same capitalist growth model that is responsible for the ongoing structural genocide. One United Nations report notes the likely failure of Africa to achieve the Millennium Development Goal related to poverty reduction:

> While Africa's high growth from 2001 to 2008 was a positive turnaround, it could not address the problem of widespread unemployment and poverty ... the region as a whole is unlikely to meet [this Millennium Development] goal without significant additional policy effort and resources. ... Another challenge for African countries is the fact that rapid economic growth does not have a substantial impact on poverty reduction. This was a notable failure in previous years despite an average 6 per cent growth rate from 2004 to 2008.[50]

And yet, having noted the failure of the growth model to reduce poverty and unemployment, the authors of the report illustrated their blind adherence to capitalist logic by suggesting that sub-Saharan Africa can regain ground lost due to the 2008 economic crisis by following the exact same discredited path:

> As they embark on economic recovery, African countries have a new opportunity to harness economic growth and reduce poverty through employment creation and social protection schemes. Strong, sustained and shared growth must be the key priority for future macroeconomic policy, given that most countries were only able to maintain stabilization during the global economic and financial crisis.[51]

Despite the fact that governments and NGOs have directed significant resources towards achieving the Millennium Development Goals, most nations in sub-Saharan Africa are unlikely to meet their objectives, for these noble efforts, while achieving improvements in some areas, are ultimately doomed to failure because they fly in the face of capitalist logic. Consequently, millions of Africans will continue to die each year from hunger and from preventable and treatable diseases in what constitutes structural genocide.

CONCLUSION

At the beginning of the twenty-first century, the United Nations Development Programme (UNDP) highlighted global inequality in a way that made apparent the consequences of structuring a social system according to the logic of capital. An additional $6 billion a year would have ensured that all children in the global South received a basic education; meanwhile, $8 billion was being spent annually on cosmetics in the United States. Similarly, Europeans spent $11 billion a year on ice cream, $2 billion more than the amount required to provide safe drinking water and adequate sanitation for everyone in the South. And the $17 billion that Americans and Europeans spend annually on pet food would easily have provided basic health care for everyone in the South.[52]

Such a degree of global inequality is not simply an unintended consequence of capitalism; it is an essential component of the global capitalist system. After all, from the perspective of capital, there are hundreds of millions of dollars in profits to be made selling cosmetics, ice cream and pet food to North Americans and Europeans, whereas there is no viable market for education and health care in the global South, where the majority of recipients simply cannot afford to pay for them. Furthermore, decisions that prioritize the production of luxuries for consumers in the global North over essentials for people in the global South are not simply callous choices; they are perfectly 'rational' decisions made according to the logic of capital. Consequently, such inequalities cannot be addressed through efforts to humanize capitalism by developing mechanisms to redistribute wealth, since such efforts will always be in conflict with the internal logic of capital. Inevitably, capital will prevail, as evidenced by the dismantling of the Keynesian policy framework and the Fordist Compact in the latter part of the twentieth century.

The inequality in power and wealth that results in structural violence is maintained through imperialist structures that ensure that crucial policymaking is conducted by liberal democratic governments in the global North and undemocratic international institutions that serve the interests of capital. As a result, there exists a democratic deficit in which a majority of the world's population have little or no say in the major decisions that directly impact their lives. The lack of input into policymaking and the inability to access land, food and life-saving drugs sentence more than 10 million people to death each year. Given that the overwhelming majority of these deaths are directly related to the inequalities resulting from the global capitalist system, they clearly meet the definition of structural violence in that they constitute human suffering caused by social structures that disproportionately benefit certain groups while preventing others from meeting their fundamental needs. And, given the massive number of deaths that annually result from this structural violence, capitalism clearly constitutes structural genocide, because the structural violence inherent in the capitalist system inflicts on a group or collectivity the conditions of life that are bringing about its physical destruction in whole or in part. In short, capitalism constitutes a class-based structural genocide that targets the poor, particularly in the global South. And it is only because birth rates in the global South have so far outpaced the number of deaths resulting from the structural genocide that capital has managed to preserve its army of surplus labour.

But how is it that certain human beings are so willing to adhere to the logic of capital when that behaviour results in a structural genocide of such magnitude? As Kovel explains,

> Because money is all that 'counts,' a peculiar heartlessness characterizes capitalists, a tough-minded and cold abstraction that will sacrifice species, whole continents (viz Africa) or inconvenient

subsets of the population (viz black urban males) who add too little to the great march of surplus value ... The presence of value screens out genuine fellow-feeling or compassion, replacing it with the calculus of profit-expansion. Never has a holocaust been carried out so impersonally.[53]

5

THE TRULY INCONVENIENT TRUTH

Because we don't think about future generations, they will never forget us.

Henrik Tikkanen

Marx argued that the dire social crisis that results from primitive accumulation and the exploitation of workers – and the consequent crisis of overproduction – would constitute a barrier that capital would ultimately not be able to overcome. He also suggested that there was a second insurmountable barrier facing capital: nature. Marx contended that capital's drive to discover new use-values in order to increase surplus value leads it to exploit natural resources throughout the world in an unsustainable manner.[1]

The logic of capital is blind to the ecological crisis that has resulted from its constant expansion in pursuit of profit because it is solely focused on accumulation. And in order to accumulate, capital requires constant economic growth. But while capital's inherent need for growth is infinite, the planet's natural resources are finite, especially when they are not exploited in a sustainable manner. Consequently, the internal contradiction in the system becomes apparent because, as Shiva notes,

> Economic growth takes place through the exploitation of natural resources. Deforestation creates growth. Mining of groundwater creates growth. Overfishing creates growth. Further economic growth cannot help regenerate the very spheres which must be destroyed for economic growth to occur. Nature shrinks as capital grows. The growth of the market cannot solve the very crisis it creates.[2]

Herein lies the fundamental contradiction between the growth-based model inherent in capitalism and ecological sustainability. As John Bellamy Foster points out, 'From an ecological perspective, of course, this system of growth at any cost, synonymous with capitalism, places the world economy in direct conflict with environmental sustainability.'[3]

That this reality has been so easy for so many to ignore rests in part with the alienated condition of workers and the related seductiveness of capitalist consumerism. Consequently, given the preponderance of anti-ecological goods produced by capital, most people in the global North become accomplices in the destruction of nature through their consumption habits. As Kovel explains,

> The commodities so introduced, say, the SUVs, are both ecodestructive and profitable; and the people who use and desire them are, because of their changed needs, themselves changed in an 'anti-ecological' direction, that is, they see capitalist life as ordained by nature, and become complicit in the ecological crisis and unable to take action against it.[4]

However, the seductiveness of capitalism's consumer culture for the alienated worker extends beyond the mere consumption of goods; it alters the very essence of human existence and its relationship to nature. Consequently, notes Kovel, 'This allows the suicidal insanity of ever-expanding accumulation to appear as natural'.[5]

THE IMPOSSIBLE DREAM

Capital sells the same consumer dream to the poor in the global South, claiming that continual economic growth will permit them to attain a materialistic standard of living equal to that enjoyed by people in the global North. This growth is to be achieved primarily through the exploitation of natural resources. But this constitutes the impossible dream because the United States, with only 4 per cent of the world's population, consumes 25 per cent of global energy production and 50 per cent of the global production of raw materials, while generating 40 per cent of the world's waste.[6] Clearly, there are not sufficient natural resources, or places on the planet to store the waste generated, to permit 7 billion people to enjoy the same materialistic standard of living as that enjoyed by 300 million people in the United States.

China's integration into the global capitalist economy and its corresponding fossil-fuel-based industrialization and economic growth make evident that the capitalist development model is not viable for the majority of people in the global South. The shift to capitalism has resulted in China experiencing increased levels of inequality similar to those present in most other countries in the global South. The economic boom has created a new urban middle class of some 200 million people who are enjoying lifestyles comparable to those of many people in the global North.[7] Meanwhile, the country's poorest province, Guizhou, has a GDP per capita lower than Ecuador, Belize and Angola.[8]

China's economic growth and the corresponding elevation of 200 million people to middle-class status through capitalist development are already raising alarm bells about global warming. It is also intensifying the conflict between imperialist powers with regard to control over the planet's dwindling natural resources, particularly fossil fuels. The Asian giant is scouring the world for increasingly scarce supplies of oil and in 2003 it surpassed Japan to become the world's second-largest consumer of oil, after the United States.[9] At the same time, China is meeting its ever-growing power needs by generating 80 per cent of its electricity from coal.[10] Like the global capitalist powers before it, China is following the traditional fossil-fuel-based capitalist development path. As Walden Bello points out, 'the elite of China as well as those of India and other rapidly developing countries are intent on reproducing the American-type overconsumption-driven capitalism' and this will inevitably result in 'ecological Armageddon'.[11]

The new middle class in China constitutes only 20 per cent of that country's total population and a mere 6 per cent of the more than 3 billion people in the global South who currently live in poverty. Given the burden placed on both the earth's resources and the environment that has resulted from elevating a mere 6 per cent of the world's impoverished population to a lifestyle equivalent to that enjoyed by many in the North, it is inconceivable that the promise of capitalist development can be fulfilled for everyone on the planet. Precisely because we do not have the four Planet Earths that would be required to sustain everyone in the world in the same material conditions enjoyed by people in the United States and other wealthy countries, the imperialist powers are intent on ensuring that their nations continue to consume a disproportionate percentage of the planet's resources. Inevitably, then, the majority of the world's population will continue to endure structural violence and structural genocide in order to maintain the status quo. As Amin points out,

> The egoism of the countries of the North was brutally expressed by former US president George W. Bush when he declared: 'The American way of life is not negotiable' ... Many in Europe and Japan feel the same way, even if they refrain from declaring it. This egoism simply means that access to these scarce natural resources will largely be denied to the countries of the South (80 per cent of humanity), whether the latter intend to use these resources in a similar way to the North, which is wasteful and dangerous, or whether they envisage more economical forms.[12]

As Mészáros observes, the contradiction evident in the dream that capital pitches to peoples of the global South highlights a fundamental contradiction in capitalism, because capital

> cannot separate 'advance' from *destruction*, nor 'progress' from *waste* – however catastrophic the results. The more it unlocks the powers of productivity, the more it must unleash the powers

of destruction; and the more it extends the volume of production, the more it must bury everything under mountains of suffocating waste. The concept of *economy* is radically incompatible with the 'economy' of capital production. It adds insult to injury by first using up with rapacious wastefulness the *limited resources* of our planet and then further aggravates the outcome by *polluting and poisoning* the human environment with its mass-produced waste and effluence.[13]

THE CLIMATE CHANGE CRISIS

One potentially catastrophic ecological consequence of capitalist development is global warming. And, as with so many other aspects of capitalism, inequality is prevalent with regard to who will be most negatively impacted by this emerging crisis. While it is the wealthy capitalist nations that are responsible for the overwhelming majority of greenhouse gas emissions that have caused global warming, it is the nations of the global South that are going to bear the brunt of the consequences because many of them are located in tropical regions that will be the most negatively impacted.

According to the UN Intergovernmental Panel on Climate Change, between 75 and 200 million people in Africa will face water shortages due to climate change by 2020 and, 'in some countries, yields from rain-fed agriculture could be reduced by up to 50%. Agricultural production, including access to food, in many African countries is projected to be severely compromised.'[14] Similarly, in Latin America, diminished water availability for human consumption and agriculture will place increasing numbers of people at risk of hunger. Meanwhile, the same report forecasts that yields from rain-fed agriculture in North America will actually increase by between 5 and 20 per cent over the next few decades.[15] This process and its human consequences in the global South are already under way, as evidenced by the aforementioned 2,000 farmers in Kenya who committed suicide in 2010 due to crop failures caused by climate change. According to Kermal Dervis of the UNDP, 'Ultimately, climate change is a threat to humanity as a whole. But it is the poor, a constituency with no responsibility for the ecological debt we are running up, who face the immediate and most severe human costs.'[16]

The fact that the poor in the global South will be disproportionately impacted by climate change, to the degree that growing numbers will not be able to meet their basic needs, will only intensify the ongoing structural genocide. It will also increase the impetus for those negatively impacted by climate change to emigrate through any means available to the wealthy nations of the global North in order to survive. The result will undoubtedly be a further entrenching of the class-based global apartheid that is emerging under capitalism as the wealthy seek to fortify themselves militarily against such an 'invasion'.

It is not surprising that capitalists have proven fiercely resistant to efforts to address the ecological crisis, particularly global warming, when those efforts promise to infringe significantly upon their ability to accumulate wealth.[17] Some simply deny that human activity contributes to climate change. Meanwhile, Al Gore and other 'green' diplomats acknowledge the problem and promote international environmental agreements and market solutions (i.e. the Kyoto Protocol and carbon trading mechanisms) that give the illusion of addressing climate change, when in reality their strategies will fail to solve the crisis. Nevertheless, solutions such as carbon trading – also known as carbon offsetting and a cap-and-trade system – are the only approaches to the crisis that capital will even contemplate, because they provide new markets in which to accumulate wealth and constitute the most palatable form of regulation. As a result, carbon trading has become the fastest-growing commodities market in the world with more than $300 billion in carbon transactions taking place between 2005 and 2010.[18]

Carbon trading allows a corporation that exceeds its permitted amount of emissions to purchase carbon credits from a company whose emissions are below its allotted amount. In other words, a corporation can pay for the right to continue to pollute excessively. Heavily polluting companies can also purchase carbon 'offsets' that allow them to continue producing greenhouse gases in excess of their permitted amount. These offsets are credits from emission-reducing projects in the global South such as the planting of trees. But given the lack of regulatory enforcement for such an international trading system, it is difficult to determine if credits for the same emission-reducing projects are being sold to multiple companies or whether the newly planted forests are being cut down after a couple of years with credits for new saplings then sold on the carbon trading market.[19] Ultimately, carbon trading is not having the desired effect and numerous studies have revealed that many of the more than 2,000 emission-reducing projects in the global South fail to achieve the promised levels of reduction.[20] As Mark Schapiro notes in reference to the trading of carbon offsets, 'That market is, in essence, an elaborate shell game, a disappearing act that nicely serves the immediate interests of the world's governments but fails to meet the challenges of our looming environmental crisis.'[21]

Some of those who acknowledge that capitalism is responsible for global warming also believe that the innovative nature of capitalism and its corresponding technological advances will ultimately address the problem. As activist Simon Butler notes, the appeal of green capitalism is obvious: 'It promises to save the planet, maintain economic growth and make lots of people lots of money. It offers the hope that there is an easy way out of the crisis – that we can halt climate change without resorting to fundamental social change.'[22]

But history suggests that green capitalism and its technological fix will not be able solve the crisis. After all, despite all the impressive technological advances of the past half-century, the extent of the ecological damage has not decreased but increased during this period. As political scientist Lee-Anne Broadhead points out,

> The heartfelt efforts of green diplomats to bridge the gap between economics and environmental issues is doomed to fail because of their acceptance of the destructive practices inherent in the growth ethic. Economic growth and the organization of international

society around the goals of efficient capital mobility and the profit margin its controllers seek are inherently anti-ecological. Any way it is looked at, the extraction of raw materials for the manufacture of goods – the demand for which in many cases has been artificially created – does not lead to an ecologically sound existence. No amount of masking the reality with talk of environmentally friendly technologies will offset the destructiveness of the growth ethic when the resounding failure of the technological fix is taken into consideration.[23]

And as Kovel notes in regard to the inevitable failure of green diplomats such as Al Gore to address global warming effectively through regulation within capitalist structures, 'This is, unfortunately, as it has to be, since global warming is an objective reminder that it is either the end of capitalism or the end of the world. ... Capital got what it wanted, and the planet got intractable global warming. Now that is a truly inconvenient truth.'[24] So, while the 'inconvenient truth' is the reality that global warming poses a threat to humanity, the 'truly inconvenient truth' is the fact that capital is incapable of effectively addressing the crisis due to the logic to which it is compelled to adhere.

CONCLUSION

Ultimately, global warming is a global problem that requires a global solution. Greenhouse gases do not recognize borders; therefore solutions implemented in individual communities or even in nations will be undermined as long as capital is permitted to continue its destructive practices elsewhere.

The unequal distribution of the planet's natural resources and the unequal consequences of climate change resulting from capitalism are not only problems for the have-nots in today's society; they will also negatively impact billions of people in the future. Capital's exploitation of the planet's resources at an unsustainable rate will ensure that future generations face an even greater struggle to meet their fundamental needs – that is, if they can meet them at all. In essence, the unequal distribution of the planet's natural resources not only results in inequality between the haves and the have-nots today; it also results in inequality between the haves of today and the have-nots of tomorrow.

Capital cannot effectively address the ecological crisis and its consequent structural genocide because to do so would require it contravening the very logic that compels it. As Kovel explains,

> Capital cannot recuperate the ecological crisis because its essential being, manifest in the 'grow or die' syndrome, is to produce such a crisis, and the only thing it really knows how to do, which is to produce according to exchange-value, is exactly the source of the crisis.... And, finally, capital's iron tendency to produce poverty along with wealth and to increase the gap between rich and poor, means that capitalist society must remain authoritarian at the core and incapable of developing the cooperative space for rationally contending with the ecological crisis.[25]

Capital's commodification and unsustainable exploitation of every aspect of nature constitutes a form of social injustice and inequality, and therefore structural violence and structural genocide against future generations, since the relatively luxurious lifestyles of a minority today are being maintained by destroying the basis of survival for our children and our grandchildren. More than 10 million people already die annually from the structural violence inherent in capitalism, and untold millions – even billions – more will perish in the future as a result of capital's anti-ecological logic. Clearly, then, if the exploitation of people and nature under capitalism is allowed to continue, the magnitude of the structural genocide will only grow, and potentially result in the extermination of the human race. As sociologist Ian Angus states, 'No society that *permits* that to happen can be called civilized. No social order that *causes* it to happen deserves to survive.'[26]

6

LEGITIMIZING THE ILLEGITIMATE

In history, in social life, nothing is fixed, rigid or definitive. And nothing ever will be.

Antonio Gramsci

Given that the capitalist system constitutes structural genocide and, as Ian Angus notes, does not deserve to survive, how has it survived? More to the point, how has this genocidal social system managed to perpetuate itself with the apparent consent of a significant portion of the world's population? In order to address this question we turn to Italian philosopher Antonio Gramsci, who argued that ruling elites gain and maintain consent by utilizing various methods to socialize the masses, and when this approach proves inadequate they resort to more overt coercion in order to preserve their hegemony.[1]

According to Gramsci, the process of social control occurs in two spheres: political society and civil society. The former consists of the state with its establishment of the rule of law and monopoly on the use of violence, while the latter involves the socialization of the masses through education, media, religion and culture, among many others things. The process of hegemony is actually conducted by intellectuals who have themselves been appropriately socialized to become the managers and operators of the capitalist system.[2] However, this method of social control is not sustainable if it is a strictly top-down process with little or no regard for the desires of the masses. Therefore hegemony allows for the introduction of reforms – when demanded – that address certain needs of the masses in order to maintain their consent. But such reforms are only implemented to the degree that they do not challenge the fundamental structures of the existing social system. This process of give and take between the ruling elites and the masses represents a form of political trench warfare that Gramsci termed a 'war of position'.[3]

In the modern state, social democracy has become the battle-ground in this 'war of position' as the popular masses – or workers – make social demands of capitalist elites, who, at least initially, resist the demands. Capitalist elites will ultimately – and reluctantly – accommodate the demands if not doing so is likely to lead to a revolt that would undermine the fundamental structures of capitalism. This process was clearly evident with capital's acceptance of the Keynesian policy framework in the global North and popular nationalism in the global South during the middle decades of the twentieth century, both of which helped undermine the influence of the more radical 'actually existing socialism' in the Soviet Union.

Through this hegemonic process, capitalist elites maintain the consent of a majority of the population, while those who with-hold their consent and demand more radical structural changes are dealt with through more overt coercive measures. Gramsci argues that the consent gained through the war of position is also influenced by the socialization process implemented by capitalist elites:

> Government with the consent of the governed – but with this con-sent organised, and not generic and vague as it is expressed in the instant of elections. The State does have and request consent, but it also 'educates' this consent, by means of political and syndical associations; these, however, are private organisms, left to the private initiative of the ruling class.[4]

This 'education' of consent instils in people the dominant capitalist ideology, thereby normalizing the values of capital and diminishing the possibility that radical challenges to the system will emerge. But when civil society – or the capitalist class – fails to maintain sufficient consent, then the state resorts to coercion to ensure the continued hegemony of capital. Coercion can involve the justice system enforcing the 'rule of law' or the use of direct physical violence by state security forces.

The process of socialization is closely related to the dominant mode of production in a society. As Gramsci explains,

> [E]very State is ethical in as much as one of its most important functions is to raise the great mass of the population to a particular cultural and moral level, a level (or type) which corresponds to the needs of the productive forces for development, and hence to the interests of the ruling classes. The school as a positive educative function, and the courts as a repressive and negative educative function, are the most important State activities in this sense: but, in reality, a multitude of other so-called private initiatives and activities tend to the same end – initiatives and activities which form the apparatus of the political and cultural hegemony of the ruling classes.[5]

In this way, the ruling elites control the discourse, thereby determining which ideological perspectives will dominate mainstream debates and which ones will be marginalized. The ideology that the hegemonic discourse of capital promotes is free-market capitalism, regardless of the contradictions that exist in the functioning of the system. According to David Roberts,

> Part of what sustains poverty and human insecurity is 'discourse dominance'. This means that neoliberalism can create the illusion of propriety by dominating debate, responses and logic. This is achieved in part by its ability to maintain that concepts like the 'free' market are valid, when the evidence shows quite clearly that the market is not free.[6]

George Lambie explains how Gramsci's theory of hegemony is relevant in the era of neoliberal globalization, thereby allowing capital to dominate the discourse globally:

LEGITIMIZING THE ILLEGITIMATE

Although Gramsci's concept of hegemony was originally applied to the formation of classes and social groups within the nation-state, it can also be extended into the international arena. In this sense, hegemony is not the power of one nation or group of nations over others, but rather 'coercion by consent' in national-level political and civil society, spilling over into international space. This is entirely consistent with the analysis of the transnationalisation of capital and productive forces, because these processes lead to the formation of political and class structures at the level where production itself operates, as can be seen by an extension of Marx's method. As the transnational elite extend their economic and productive power into global space, they also carry their domination over political, social and class relations into the same arena. In this context Gramsci's notion of hegemony, as the exercise of elite power over national civil society in the form of consensual domination, can be extended to refer to a global configuration.[7]

THE ART OF CONSENT

The roles played by the education system and the media – particularly corporate media – in the hegemonic process have been crucial. Schools instil in children at an early age the values preferred by capital, and the media reinforce those values through their news coverage and entertainment programming. An important aspect of the hegemonic process under capitalism has been to keep people distracted while simultaneously convincing them that they are free and that they live in the most democratic of societies. To a large degree, the hegemonic discourse succeeds because, as Alan Maass explains,

> we're continually exposed to various institutions that are in the business of reinforcing these myths and prejudices. The mass media are one example. ... Or take the education system, which is plainly designed to encourage conformity. Except for the minority of students being trained to rule society, the experience of school is usually alienating. Students are taught to compete against each other from Kindergarten and even before. The underlying objective is to encourage students to accept the conditions they see around them rather than challenge them.[8]

f education, particularly in secondary schools,
1 regimented. Students adhere to strict class
.ssroom structures that usually require students
. an orderly fashion in rows. Students quickly learn to
..ccept a hierarchical system with the teacher constituting an
authority figure who wields significant power, particularly with
regard to the issuance of grades. The use of examinations is
an effective tool to induce conformity, not only with regard to
knowledge gained through the rote memorization of facts rather
than critically analysing concepts, but also in behaviour. As
French philosopher Michel Foucault explained, 'The examination
combines the techniques of an observing hierarchy and those of
a normalizing judgement. It is a normalizing gaze, a surveillance
that makes it possible to qualify, to classify, and to punish.'[9]
Ultimately, once the education system has produced young citizens that have internalized the values of capitalism – such as
unquestioningly accepting liberal governance and the right to
private property (i.e. private ownership of the means of production) among others things – capital gains their consent rather
effortlessly. As a result, most people then enter the workplace
having internalized the values and behaviours in the classroom
required to ensure that they conform to the appropriate rules
and hierarchical structures at work.

The mainstream media have also played a crucial role in both
gaining and maintaining the consent of a significant portion of
the population. The mainstream media have become increasingly
concentrated in the hands of fewer and fewer corporations that
adhere to the logic of capital and, therefore, have a vested interest
in maintaining the political and economic status quo. According
to Robert McChesney, 'Following the logic of accumulation, the
commercial press system became less competitive and ever more
clearly the domain of wealthy individuals, who usually had the
political views associated with their class.'[10] Consequently, there
is an aversion in the commercial news media to engaging in hard-
hitting investigative journalism that challenges the fundamental
structures of capitalism. The media primarily reflect the views of

those in power, and a critique of those in power only emerges when there are differences in opinion between factions of the ruling elite – for example, between the Republicans and the Democrats in the United States. The media then present both elite views under the banner of objectivity – each of which contains a critique of the opposing elite view but not of the system itself.

This process occurs because 'professional' journalists are too often overly dependent on official sources. For their part, government officials are fully aware of the mainstream media's over-reliance on official sources, and routinely hold press conferences or invite reporters to public events in order to present them with a prepackaged story. Inevitably, the official line dominates the published account. Government officials realize that the media will obediently cover these events because they provide convenient stories for reporters working under tight deadlines. They know that if they keep the media occupied daily with prepackaged stories that portray government policy in a positive light, then reporters may be too busy to conduct deeper investigative journalism. As McChesney indicates,

> The limitations of this reliance upon official sources are self-evident. It gives those in political office (and, to a lesser extent, business) considerable power to set the news agenda by what they speak about and, just as important, what they keep quiet about. When a journalist dares to raise an issue that no official source is talking about, he or she is accused of being unprofessional, and attempting to introduce his or her own biases into the news. ... Journalists find themselves where they cannot antagonize their sources too much, or they might get cut off and become ineffectual.[11]

There is perhaps no clearer example of this process than the uncritical coverage of the lead-up to the war in Iraq provided by *New York Times* reporter Judith Miller. When asked why her articles often did not include the views of experts sceptical of the Bush administration's claims of weapons of mass destruction, Miller replied: 'My job isn't to assess the government's information and be an independent intelligence analyst myself. My job is to tell readers of the *New York Times* what the government thought of Iraq's arsenal.'¹² Such an approach reduces journalists to little more than stenographers for government officials rather than reporters investigating a meaningful issue related to the public interest.

Miller's uncritical approach was not unique; the official line dominated much of the mainstream media's coverage, resulting in one in five Americans believing that Iraq was directly involved in the 9/11 terrorist attacks, with 13 per cent believing they had been given conclusive evidence. A further 36 per cent believed that Iraq provided substantial support to al-Qaeda.¹³ And so, with 56 per cent of Americans believing that Iraq was directly or indirectly involved in the 9/11 attacks – neither of which was true – the Bush administration had gained sufficient consent from the US public to initiate a war that most of the world's population believed to be immoral and that the secretary general of the United Nations later deemed to be illegal.¹⁴

Media corporations that adhere to the logic of capital have a vested interest in preserving a social system that serves the interests of capital. Within that system, their objective is to maximize profits, which requires achieving ever-higher levels of viewership or readership. As a result, news coverage has become just another form of entertainment that seeks to appeal to as many people as possible. As such it focuses on sensational stories related to violent crime, traffic accidents, celebrity gossip and human interest stories that help depoliticize and distract the masses from the real issues that impact their lives. And to the degree to which the news and entertainment media do address any issues relevant to people's lives, they are presented in a form that reinforces the values at the core of capitalism, such as individualism, competition and consumerism, thereby perpetuating the hegemonic discourse of capital and allowing capital accumulation to continue unhindered. According to Alan Maass,

> Watch cable TV news, and you'll see sensationalized stories about crime and violence or titillating celebrity gossip – while discussions about the real issues that affect people's lives get shortchanged. The poor are stereotyped and scapegoated, while the wealth and power

of the rich are celebrated. Even shows meant as entertainment tend to reinforce the conventional wisdom.[15]

The conscious omission of Marxist and other alternative perspectives in both education and the media allows capital to achieve 'consensual domination'. The marginalization of critical perspectives results not only from the dominant role played by capitalist elites in the socialization process, but also from reformist sectors that seek to achieve moderate change from within the system. As a result, liberal democracy and capitalism are legitimized while the values they promote are viewed as common sense. Meanwhile, those who challenge the prevailing order are easily dismissed as 'radicals' or 'extremists'.

Another important component in the success of the hegemonic discourse of capital – in which media and education have also played crucial roles – has been its ability to obscure the historical links between wealth accumulation in the global North and misery in the global South. As Paul Farmer notes,

> Erasing history is perhaps the most common explanatory sleight-of-hand relied upon by the architects of structural violence. Erasure or distortion of history is part of the process of desocialization necessary for the emergence of hegemonic accounts of what happened and why. ... And there are certain times, such as now, in which exploring the historical roots of a problem is not a popular process. There is not always much support for laying bare the fretwork of entrenched structures that promise more misery.[16]

Similarly, Sue McGregor describes the disconnect that exists between consumers in the global North and producers in the South, as well as how that disconnect is ensured,

> Under the spell of consumerism, few people give thought to whether their consumption habits produce class inequality, alienation, or repressive power, i.e., structural violence. ... We teach children capitalistic consumerism, yet tell them nothing about the lives of the workers who slave to assemble designer clothing, toys, and electronics; nor the animals that suffered to create fashion or food; nor the environmental impact of the trash we create. And, by no means do we tell them that these situations are inextricably linked.[17]

It is not surprising that the hegemonic discourse of capital has proven particularly effective in the global North. Perhaps most startling is the degree of success that the discourse has achieved in the global South. As Samir Amin explains, the discourse related to neoliberal globalization has strengthened

> the general embrace of the ideology of consumption and the idea that progress is measured by the quantitative growth of consumption. ... The peoples of the peripheries, who are for the most part deprived of access to acceptable levels of consumption and blinded by aspirations to consume like the opulent North, are losing consciousness of the fact that the logic of historical capitalism makes the extension of this model to the entire globe impossible.[18]

Some sectors of contemporary 'civil society', which includes NGOs, charitable organizations, unions and social movements, fall into the 'reformist political tradition' referred to by Mészáros and play an important role in maintaining the hegemony of capital. In essence, they constitute what Gramsci called the 'private initiatives and activities ... which form the apparatus of the political and cultural hegemony of the ruling classes'. Slavoj Žižek argues that NGOs headed by Bill Gates, George Soros and others of their ilk fulfil the hegemonic role described by Gramsci. First, these individuals generate huge wealth in the private sector and then promote charity as the solution to the structural violence inherent in the very system they utilized to get rich, thereby suggesting that equality and sustainability can be achieved under capitalism. Žižek argues that this is an age-old practice:

> Good old Andrew Carnegie employed a private army brutally to suppress organised labour in his steelworks and then distributed large parts of his wealth to educational, artistic, and humanitarian causes. A man of steel, he proved he had a heart of gold. In the same way, [Gates, Soros and others] give away with one hand what they first took with the other. ... Soros stands for the most ruthless financial speculative exploitation combined with its counter-agent, humanitarian concern about the catastrophic social consequences of an unbridled market economy. ... The two faces of Bill Gates parallel the two faces of Soros. The cruel businessman destroys or buys out competitors, aims at virtual monopoly, employs all the tricks of

the trade to achieve his goals. ... Charity is the humanitarian mask hiding the face of economic exploitation.[19]

Žižek argues that the same strategy is utilized by governments of wealthy nations in the global North through the disbursement of foreign aid: 'In a superego blackmail of gigantic proportions, the developed countries "help" the undeveloped with aid, credits, and so on, and thereby avoid the key issue, namely their complicity in and co-responsibility for the miserable situation of the undeveloped.'[20]

Regardless of whether it is humanitarian aid provided by NGOs, community services offered as part of corporate social responsibility programmes, or foreign aid disbursed by governments of wealthy nations, the decisions that impact the lives of billions of people in the global South are still being made in the imperialist countries of the North. Therefore the power and the wealth still ultimately reside in the global North, ensuring a continuance of inequality and social injustice. Ultimately, the impression created is that the peoples of the dominant capitalist powers are 'generously' donating a portion of 'their' wealth to 'help' alleviate the massive human suffering in the 'underdeveloped' nations of the global South.

The reality is, in fact, the opposite. The total of all the loans and aid provided by the global North to the global South is less than the amount of money that flows in the opposite direction in foreign debt payments alone. Between 1998 and 2002, for example, nations in the global South received $855 billion in aid and loans while sending $922 billion in debt payments to financial institutions in the global North – a net gain of $67 billion in favour of the North.[21] Debt repayment does not constitute the only manner in which wealth flows disproportionately from the South to the North. The brain drain inhibits potential for development in nations of the global South while benefiting the economies and the people of the North. For instance, the brain drain of doctors from African nations to wealthy nations has resulted in a loss of more than $2 billion in health-care investment for the nine sub-Saharan African countries with the highest rates of

HIV/AIDS. In contrast, the USA, Britain, Canada and Australia have saved more than $4.5 billion by having to train fewer doctors than they require. As a result, sub-Saharan Africa, which bears 24 per cent of the global burden of disease, has only 2 per cent of the global supply of doctors. According to a 2011 study, 'Many wealthy destination countries, which also train fewer doctors than are required, depend on immigrant doctors to make up the shortfall. In this way developing countries are effectively paying to train staff who then support the health services of developed countries.'[22] In Canada more than 22 per cent of doctors are foreign-trained, with the principal source countries located in sub-Saharan Africa.[23]

Additionally, the privatization of profitable state-owned companies results in wealth accumulation for those multinational corporations based in the North that purchase them and diminished revenues for governments in the global South, making it more difficult for them to service their debts and to provide adequate education, health care and other social services to their populations. But these realities, which illustrate the degree to which it is the global North that is dependent on the global South, remain hidden due to the effectiveness of the dominant hegemonic discourse, in which capital's philanthropic endeavours play an important role.

Through education, the media and private initiatives, the state and capitalist elites control the hegemonic discourse, and thereby gain the consent of a sufficient portion of the global population to provide capitalism with a veneer of legitimacy. The intent of this hegemonic discourse is to convince people that capitalism provides them with the greatest opportunity to live free in a democratic society, which will ultimately allow them to improve their material condition. The hegemonic discourse, in part through the philanthropic endeavours of capital, also seeks to socialize people into believing capitalism is a humane social system that provides opportunities for individuals who are willing to work hard. In this manner, the hegemonic discourse creates a disconnect in the minds of people with regard to the success of an individual and the related suffering of many others. As Ernesto 'Che' Guevara noted,

> That is how it is painted by capitalist propagandists who purport to draw a lesson from the example of Rockefeller ... about the possibilities of individual success. The amount of poverty and suffering required for a Rockefeller to emerge, and the amount of depravity entailed in the accumulation of a fortune of such magnitude, are left out of the picture, and it is not always possible for the popular forces to expose this clearly.[24]

In the global North, where the majority of people enjoy a middle-class lifestyle, 'petty bourgeois' attitudes have come to predominate.[25] Amin argues, 'The "petty bourgeois" is an individual who is not bourgeois (they do not have access to capital, even at a modest level), but they believe themselves to be so.'[26] This occurs because the hegemonic discourse of capital has resulted in the majority of people internalizing the values of capitalism: individualism, self-interest and competition. In fact, these values have been internalized to the degree that many view them as human nature. But nothing could be further from the truth. For if these individualistic values constitute human nature, then how do we explain thousands of years of human beings organizing themselves collectively in one form or another – and continuing to do so in many indigenous communities? Kovel asks,

> For if capital were natural, why has it only occupied the last 500 years of a record that goes back for hundreds of thousands? More to the point, why did it have to be imposed through violence wherever it set down rule? And most importantly, why does it have to be continually maintained through violence, and continuously reimposed on each generation through an enormous apparatus of indoctrination?[27]

As a result of the hegemonic discourse of capital, most people's world-views currently reflect the values of capital. Gaining the consent of a significant portion of the population has proven to be a relatively easy task in the wealthy nations of the global North, where the majority of people benefit from capitalism's structural genocide to a sufficient degree that they can escape their alienated condition through consumption. The hegemonic discourse has also successfully shielded consumers in the global North from the reality that their material comfort is intrinsically linked to the structural genocide being perpetrated against tens of millions of people in the global South.

THE ART OF COERCION

The greatest resistance to capital has occurred in the global South, which consequently has been forced to endure coercion through military interventions. In the era of neoliberal globalization, coercion through the rule of law and direct physical violence has taken on international dimensions in institutions such as the WTO, the ICC, the UN Security Council, NATO and even unilateral military actions on the part of the USA. When nations do not abide by the international rules established by capital, then the first form of coercion that seeks to bring them back into the fold is economic sanctions, which often result in structural violence being perpetrated against the targeted population due to a shortage of basic necessities such as food and medicines.

If this coercive measure fails, then the 'rogue' nation will be subjected to direct physical violence in the form of military intervention or support for a *coup d'état* carried out by allied domestic elites. Naturally, such military endeavours are not presented for what they really are: the coercion of the peoples of the global South in defence of capital. Rather, they are more often than not presented as 'democracy promotion' or 'humanitarian intervention'; modern-day colloquialisms that essentially retain the same meaning as the colonial-era expression 'civilizing the natives'.

The list of US interventions since World War II is impressive, having targeted Mohammad Mossadegh in Iran, Jacobo Arbenz in Guatemala, Fidel Castro in Cuba, Salvador Allende in Chile, the Sandinistas in Nicaragua, and Jean-Bertrand Aristide in Haiti, among many others – as well as the ongoing antagonism towards Hugo Chávez in Venezuela. All of these leaders, most of whom were democratically elected, have one thing in common: in one way or another, they challenged the hegemony of capital.

As of 2011, the United States had economic sanctions in place against more than a dozen nations and was conducting air strikes against six countries – Afghanistan, Pakistan, Iraq, Yemen, Libya and Somalia – in addition to having combat troops on the ground in two of these nations.[28] While there are arguably legitimate human rights justifications for many such interventions, such justifications only seem to apply to nations that constitute some form of challenge to the interests of capital and not to those repressive regimes (Saudi Arabia, Kazakhstan, Nigeria, etc.) that serve the interests of capital.

It is also important to note that the massive military expenditures of the United States not only allow it to defend the hegemony of capital through coercive measures that target 'rogue' nations such as those listed above, but that they also support the military–industrial complex that produces this military capacity. The military–industrial complex serves as yet another mechanism through which capitalists can achieve capital accumulation. This process of capital accumulation exposes the ultimate irrationality and even lunacy of the capitalist system through its production of the means (i.e. nuclear weapons) by which we can efficiently exterminate the human race. In short, war constitutes a widening of the spheres of production and circulation for capital.

CONCLUSION

Despite the dominance of capital over the hegemonic discourse – and despite repeated attempts at coercion through economic sanctions and military interventions – many people in the global South continue to challenge the hegemony of capital by demanding a new social system that emphasizes the social well-being of all instead of profit for a few. In other words, they are demanding a social system that is not dominated by exploitation, social injustice, inequality, structural violence and structural genocide. In reference to this alternative society, Samir Amin has stated: 'I do not see any name for this other than socialism.'[29] It is to this alternative that we turn in the next chapter.

7

THE SOCIALIST ALTERNATIVE

> There is no other definition of socialism valid for us than that
> of the abolition of the exploitation of man by man.
>
> *Ernesto 'Che' Guevara*

Capitalism is in crisis. There are no more iron curtains to
tear down in order to expand capital's spheres of production
and circulation. In fact, under neoliberal globalization, capital
has penetrated virtually every corner of the globe in its never-
ending quest to accumulate. It has even penetrated the immaterial world by introducing intellectual property rights to a
degree never before imaginable. This capitalist expansion has
constituted a class-based genocidal process that is inherently
unsustainable from an ecological perspective. In the face of
such crisis, Mészáros argues that what is at stake is nothing
less than 'humanity's potential self-destruction at this juncture
of historical development, through both military conflagration
and the ongoing destruction of nature'.[1]

THERE IS A REVOLUTIONARY ALTERNATIVE

Despite this reality, the hegemonic discourse of capital has
convinced many people – even on the left – that there is no

alternative, and that capitalism is the only viable social system. As a result, notes sociologist Colin Cremin, many progressives recognize 'capitalism as one of a number of explanations for crises of economy and ecology while rejecting alternative models to capitalism as implausible and undesirable'.[2] Consequently, rather than recognizing capitalism as *the* primary cause of the economic and ecological crisis and therefore struggling to abolish it, many progressives instead work to humanize capitalism by seeking to achieve change within a genocidal system.

But there is a revolutionary alternative to capitalism; and it *is* possible for humankind to live in a more democratic, egalitarian and sustainable society. However, as Mészáros explains, such an alternative requires a

> Marxian program of radically restructuring, from top to bottom, the totality of social institutions, the industrial, political, and ideological conditions of present-day existence, and the whole manner of being of men and women repressed by the alienated and reified conditions of commodity-society.[3]

Such a radical restructuring rules out any possibility that the capitalist system can be reformed, because any reform in favour of human need that results in diminished profits will always be in conflict with the internal logic of capital. Those who advocate for compelling capital to serve the greater good – instead of abolishing capital – are suggesting that we remain within the capitalist system and that we simply humanize it. But, as Žižek states, 'If there ever was a utopian idea, this is surely the one.'[4]

The ultimate failure of the Keynesian policy framework during the middle decades of the twentieth century made evident the futility of attempting to regulate capitalism as a means to distribute wealth more equally and achieve social justice. Therefore, as Mészáros notes in reference to the struggle against capital in general and the economic crisis of 2008 in particular,

> One of the understandable, but ultimately self-defeating, illusions we have to guard against is any form of *neo-Keynesianism*, including

so-called *left-Keynesianism*. The calls for its revival today are under-
standable because they correspond to *the line of least resistance* to
which the personifications of capital can *temporarily* agree under
the circumstances of a major crisis.[5]

It is also unrealistic to think that liberal democracy, under
which the Keynesian policy framework was implemented, could
be a venue for achieving radical social transformation. According
to John Holloway, liberal democratic systems fail to reflect the
wishes of the popular masses and help to ensure the dominance
of capital:

> Representation is part of the general process of separation which
> is capitalism. It is completely wrong to think of representative
> government as a challenge to capitalist rule or even as a potential
> challenge to capital. Representative democracy is not opposed to
> capital: rather it is an extension of capital, it projects the principle
> of capitalist domination into our opposition to capital.[6]

Similarly, under neoliberalism, the dramatic expansion of the
so-called social economy to fill the void created by the state's
abdication of its social responsibilities in the post-Keynesian
era has also failed to address the structural genocide effectively.
The social economy seeks reforms within the capitalist system
through the promotion of a separate 'social' economy to deal with
those social and environmental issues that the market cannot effectively address. The social economy is dominated by volunteer-
based community groups and entrepreneurial not-for-profit and
for-profit organizations, with one of the more prominent entities
being 'social enterprises'. According to the British government,
'A social enterprise is a business with primarily social objectives
whose surpluses are principally reinvested for that purpose in
the business or in the community, rather than being driven by
the need to maximise profit for shareholders and owners.'[7]

The social economy approach to addressing social problems
highlights two issues. First, the growing need for social economy
enterprises under capitalism makes evident the failure of conventional profit-driven capitalist ventures to ensure that the basic

needs of everyone are met. And second, the acceptance of the broader conventional market economy by proponents of the social economy helps legitimize both capitalism and liberal democracy. At the end of the day, the social economy is a market-based solution in which the logic of capital rather than just 'social need' dramatically influences programming decisions. Ironically, many proponents of the social economy seek independence from the state while remaining dependent on government funding and their ability to influence state policies, which often limit their effectiveness in a liberal democracy where the state's objectives are to serve the interests of capital and are, therefore, at odds with the goals of proponents of the social economy.

Ultimately, the social economy approach amounts to little more than the application of a band-aid in a futile effort to stem the flow of blood gushing from an appendage severed by the brutality of capitalism. This is not to suggest that the work of those engaged in the social economy is not important, since it helps people and communities in the here and now and, despite its reformist approach, promotes some of the values essential for a more democratic and sustainable alternative to capitalism.

It is not surprising that social democratic and social economy approaches have failed to address effectively the gross social inequalities – and by extension the structural violence and structural genocide – that exist globally under capitalism precisely because, as Mises noted, they remain 'subject to the sovereignty of the market'. After all, given that the capitalist system constitutes structural genocide, how can mere reforms applied to a genocidal system bring about an end to structural genocide? The answer is, of course, that they cannot. Consequently, such a system must be dismantled and an alternative social system brought into existence. Samir Amin does not see any name other than socialism for a more humane alternative to capitalism. But how is one to define socialism? What might it look like? These are among the most pressing questions of our time. In fact, they are the crucial questions that humankind must answer if we are to avoid entering into a state of barbarism, or even extinction, after capitalism implodes due to its own internal contradictions. After all, in reality, the issue is not a lack of alternatives to capitalism, but rather that there is no alternative to socialism if the human race is to perpetuate itself in a humane and sustainable manner.

DEFINING SOCIALISM

As Alan Maass succinctly stated, 'Socialism is based on a simple idea – that the resources of society be used to meet people's needs.'[8] In other words, at the heart of socialism is the impulse to further the development of all people in a sustainable manner, as opposed to the concept of development that exists under capitalist logic, which is to establish the conditions that allow capital to maximize profits for the benefit of a small minority based on the exploitation of the majority and the destruction of nature. Therefore, any transformation to socialism must involve the emancipation of both human beings and nature.

Michael Lebowitz suggests that the transition to socialism is a 'process of substituting for the logic of capital the logic of human development'.[9] To that end, Lebowitz has proposed a 'Charter for Human Development', which contains some fundamental principles around which to structure a socialist society:

1. Everyone has the right to share in the social heritage of human beings – and equal right to the use and benefits of the products of the social brain and the social hand – in order to be able to develop his or her full potential.
2. Everyone has the right to be able to develop their full potential and capacities through democracy, participation, and protagonism in the workplace and society – a process in which these subjects of activity have the precondition of the health and education that permit them to make full use of this opportunity.
3. Everyone has the right to live in a society in which human beings and nature can be nurtured – a society in which we

can develop our full potential in communities based upon cooperation and solidarity.[10]

Exactly what form these principles might take in any given society will be influenced by many factors. Therefore the precise structure of socialism – and the path taken to achieve it – will necessarily differ from community to community and country to country. There is no blueprint; no one-size-fits-all model. However, it is crucial that any socialist alternative fundamentally address the alienation experienced by workers under capitalism, in which the only outlet for achieving some degree of fulfilment is the immediate – and temporary – gratification offered by consumerism. Therefore there are two interconnected components that are crucial to establishing a socialist society that adheres to the principles formulated by Lebowitz and that addresses the alienated state of the masses: participatory democracy and social ownership of the means of production. A participatory democracy provides people with a meaningful voice in all of the major decisions that impact their lives, with an essential aspect of that participatory democracy being the social ownership of the means of production. In other words, socialism requires democratic control over every sphere of life, including the workplace – where many people spend most of their waking hours.

Only through the social ownership of the means of production within a broader participatory democracy can a truly democratic society be achieved. This stands in contrast to capitalist society in which democracy – in a limited representative form – exists solely in the political sphere and the economy is managed in an authoritarian manner according to the logic of capital – which requires that workers surrender their democratic rights and most of their individual freedoms as soon as they enter the workplace. Most people who have internalized capitalist concepts of democracy would never tolerate a dictatorship in the political sphere, regardless of how benevolent it may be. And yet, as employees, they unquestioningly tolerate dictatorship in the economic sphere of their lives, whether benevolent or not.

Even in a small business with the most considerate of owners, there still exists inequality in both wealth and power that makes evident the dominance of one class (the owner) over another (the worker), regardless of the salary earned by the latter. Furthermore, those who advocate for small privately owned businesses serving local markets instead of large corporations are in denial regarding the power of the logic of capital, which compels a successful entity to grow and expand. And for those rare small-business owners who manage to withstand the compulsion to expand a successful venture and instead remain locally based, this has been achieved in spite of the system rather than because of it. Furthermore, such small-business owners often find themselves almost as voiceless and powerless as workers in the face of the massive wealth and political influence wielded by corporations in a liberal democracy. Consequently, Amin argues that it is essential that a socialist society 'associate the socialisation of economic management and the deepening of the democratisation of society. There will be no socialism without democracy, but equally no democratic advance outside a socialist perspective'.[11]

So what would social ownership of the means of production and a participatory democracy entail? First, and crucially, it would require recapturing the commons from capital. As Kovel explains,

> The history of capital may be viewed as a never-ending battle to take over collective and organic relationships and replace these with commodity relationships, which is to say, to create private property by destroying the *Commons*, and to embed this in the accumulation of capital. ... It is the continually shifting form of that history of class struggle in which Marx recognized the history of human society itself. It comes into fruition in a million particular battles, each of which is there to be addressed and all of which are there to be combined into a transformative vision of the new world.[12]

Therefore the transformative vision of the new post-capitalist world must involve recapturing the commons through the implementation of social ownership of the means of production in all sectors: manufacturing, agricultural and service. According to Lebowitz,

> Social ownership of the means of production is critical ... because it is the only way to ensure that our communal, social productivity is directed to the free development of all rather than used to satisfy the private goals of capitalists, groups of producers, or state bureaucrats.[13]

Social ownership of the means of production could consist of state ownership. However, under such a system, it would be essential that the workers manage the production process in order to avoid the establishment of hierarchical structures in which the state simply replaces the capitalist as the owner, thereby resulting in a form of state capitalism, which is essentially what occurred in the 'actually existing socialism' of the Soviet Union. Kovel argues that

> one must unequivocally say that 'actually existing socialism' never passed over the threshold of restoring to the producers control over the means of production. In other words, it did not live up to the stirring words of the *Communist Manifesto*, that the goal is for society to become 'an association in which the free development of each is the condition for the free development of all'.[14]

Another model of social ownership consists of worker-owned enterprises. In this instance it is crucial that there be some overarching guidance through participatory democratic processes that ensures that such entities produce in accordance with the needs of society rather than simply replacing competition for profit between privately owned businesses with competition for profit between cooperatively owned enterprises. Ultimately, management of the workplace – whether state-owned or worker-owned – must be democratic and carried out in coordination with the broader community to ensure that these enterprises serve the needs of both the immediate community and society at large. As Mészáros argues, 'The radical novelty of our condition of existence, in the present historical epoch, is that there can be no lasting success in the struggle for humanity's survival without the establishment of a *social order* based on *substantive equality* as its central orienting principle on the terrain of both *production* and *distribution*'.[15]

As for participatory democracy, it must deepen citizen engagement in decision-making beyond the mere formality of casting ballots in elections held every few years. In order to be truly effective, political institutions cannot be authoritarian, as has been the case in liberal democracies and under the 'actually existing socialism' of the past century; rather, they must be responsive to the will of the people. It was the top-down nature of policymaking – and the related lack of participatory democracy – that lay at the root of the failures of 'actually existing socialism' in the twentieth century. As Lambie points out,

> Stalin's crude methods to enforce socialism from above were repeated by other Communists of the twentieth century including Mao, whose 'Cultural Revolution' led to the deaths of millions of Chinese. This in turn influenced barbarous regimes such as that of Pol Pot in Cambodia, which attempted similar 'purifications' of society in the name of socialism.[16]

Therefore, explains Marta Harnecker, the role of political institutions must be to 'facilitate, not to supersede. We have to fight to eliminate any sign of verticalism which cancels out people's initiative because popular participation is not something that can be decreed from above.'[17] Similarly, Lebowitz suggests that socialism requires

> a process in which people are involved in making the decisions which affect them at every relevant level (i.e. their neighbourhoods, communities and society as a whole) ... Through their involvement in this democratic decision making, people transform both their circumstances and themselves – they produce themselves as subjects in the new society.[18]

Ultimately, these two components – social ownership of the means of production and participatory democracy – are intimately linked, because, as Ellen Meiksins Wood notes, 'while liberal democracy can be compatible with capitalism precisely because it leaves production relations intact, socialist democracy by definition entails the transformation of production relations.'[19] In essence, participatory democracy cannot exist as long as people lack a meaningful voice in the economic sphere of their lives.

According to Marx, the structures of capitalism reduce the labour of the worker to a mere commodity and the resulting state of alienation stifles virtually all self-development. The inequalities in power and wealth that are inherent in capitalism ensure that most human beings will never reach their full potential. A new society, including a social process of production, that emphasizes the full personal development of each and every person is required if human beings are to develop fully as individuals. In such a society, explains Marx,

> It will be seen how in place of the *wealth* and *poverty* of political economy come the *rich human being* and rich *human need*. The *rich* human being is simultaneously the human being *in need of a totality* of human manifestations of life – the man in whom his own realisation exists as an inner necessity, as *need*.[20]

Similarly, Lebowitz suggests that such a shift in self-development results from, and contributes to, a society rooted in cooperation and solidarity. In such a socialist society,

> Inherited elements such as the emphasis upon individual self-interest are subordinated by developing *a new social rationality* – one that focuses upon the community and its needs and encourages the development of new social norms based upon cooperation and solidarity among members of society. The combination of that focus and the creation of communal institutions that democratically identify communal needs and coordinate productive activity to satisfy those needs is at the center of the new socialist common sense.[21]

But where is such a revolutionary transformation likely to occur? In his early years, Marx's overly deterministic approach led him to believe that it would be industrialized workers in countries in the advanced stage of capitalism that would lead such a revolution. However, Marx later shifted his position after recognizing that workers in wealthy capitalist nations often sided with capital against immigrant labour and in defending imperialist adventures in order to protect the limited material gains they had made.[22] Consequently, instead of viewing the industrial proletariat as the only possible revolutionary vanguard, Marx came to see traditional agrarian, non-capitalist societies living under the yolk of imperialism as crucial allies to Western labour – and even as potential catalysts of international revolution. Sociologist Kevin B. Anderson argues that Marx's later works 'were not incidental to Marx's theorization of capitalism, but part of a complex analysis of the global order of his time'.[23] As Anderson explains,

> Marx's proletariat was not only white and European, but also encompassed Black labor in America, as well as Irish, not considered 'white' at the time either by the dominant cultures of Britain and North America. Moreover, as capitalist modernity penetrated into Russia and Asia, undermining the precapitalist social orders of these societies, new possibilities for revolutionary change would, he held, emerge from these new locations. Here, his hopes centered on the communal forms of the villages of India and Russia, which he saw as possible new *loci* of resistance to capital.[24]

It was during the last five years of his life that Marx most clearly deviated from the historical determinism so prevalent in *The Communist Manifesto* and other early works as he analysed the potential for revolution in agrarian societies, particularly Russia. In reference to this later work, Anderson notes: 'Marx poses more explicitly here than elsewhere the possibility that noncapitalist societies might move directly to socialism on the basis of their indigenous communal forms, without first passing through the stage of capitalism.'[25] In fact, Marx directly warned of the danger Russia faced if it failed to engage in a revolutionary transformation prior to becoming a capitalist nation when he stated, 'I have come to the conclusion that if Russia continues along the pathway she has followed since 1861, she will lose the finest chance ever offered by history to a people and undergo all the fateful vicissitudes of the capitalist regime.'[26]

Marx's anthropological studies during his later years led him to conclude ultimately that agrarian societies in Latin America, Africa and Asia that consisted of communal systems of ownership and production could achieve socialism without first passing through the capitalist stage of development. However, in order to avoid such a transition simply resulting in what Marx termed 'crude communism', it was crucial that these new socialist societies incorporate the technological and scientific advances developed in other nations under capitalism. Furthermore, Marx suggested that revolutionary transformation in non-capitalist societies on the periphery could actually be the catalyst for revolution in advanced capitalist nations. Marx emphasized, however, that such a revolution in nations on the periphery of the capitalist system needed to occur in conjunction with one in the nations at the core. Echoing Marx's views, Mészáros also emphasizes the necessity for revolution to occur ultimately in nations both on the periphery and at the centre of the global capitalist system:

> The final point to stress is the necessarily global determination of the alternative system of social control, in confrontation with the global system of capital as a mode of control. In the world as it has been – and is still being – transformed by the immense power of capital, the social institutions constitute a closely interlocking system. Thus, there is no hope for *isolated, partial* successes – only for *global* ones – however paradoxical this might sound.[27]

Clearly, in the early twenty-first century virtually every nation on the planet has been incorporated into the global capitalist system. Nevertheless, there still exist societies, particularly in the global South, that have retained significant communal forms of social organization, particularly at the community level. These societies could potentially not only achieve a revolutionary transformation to socialism without passing through the advanced stage of capitalism, but also serve as the catalyst for revolution in nations in the global North. In fact, none of the major social upheavals of the past century occurred in an advanced capitalist nation. Therefore, in all likelihood, as Marx suggested, it will be those societies in the global South that exist on the periphery of the capitalist system that will be at the forefront of any revolution. Like Marx before him, Amin also sees the global South as the focal point of any revolutionary transformation to socialism:

> I situate the new agrarian question at the heart of the challenge for the 21st century. The dispossession of the peasantry (in Asia, Africa and Latin America) is the major contemporary form of the tendency towards pauperisation (in the sense which Marx ascribed to this law), linked to accumulation. ... I deduce from this that the development of the struggles in the peasant societies of the South (almost half of humankind) and the responses to these struggles will largely determine the capacity or otherwise of workers and the peoples to progress on the road to constructing an authentic civilisation, liberated from the domination of capital.[28]

Latin America is arguably the region where the liberatory struggle against capital has been most prominent during the first decade of the twenty-first century. It was the first region to be ravaged by neoliberal globalization during the 1970s and 1980s and, not coincidentally, has thus far posited the most radical response to the so-called free-trade model. As Mészáros notes,

> The social and intellectual ferment in Latin America promises more for the future, in this respect, than what we can find for the time being in capitalistically advanced countries. This is understandably so, because the need for a truly radical change is that much more pressing in Latin America than in Europe and the United States. 'Modernization' and 'development' proved to be empty promises, and for the people at the receiving end of the policies a complete failure. It remains true that socialism, as an alternative social reproductive order, must qualify as a universally viable approach, embracing also the most developed capitalist areas of the world, including the United States. ... Given the massive inertia generated by capital's vested interests in the privileged capitalist countries and reformist labor's consensual complicity in their self-serving

development, a triggering social upheaval is much more likely to take place in Latin America than in the United States or Western Europe, with far-reaching implications for the rest of the world.[29]

Of the Latin American nations currently engaged in a transformation to socialism, it is Bolivia – due to the country's large indigenous population – that most closely reflects Marx's concept of a society in which communal forms of social organization remain prominent. Venezuela, in contrast, faces a much greater challenge because the individualistic culture of capitalism is more deeply entrenched due to that country's relatively small indigenous population and the dominant role played by US imperialism during the twentieth century related to the country's vast oil reserves. Meanwhile, Cuba constitutes the most advanced of the socialist experiments currently taking place in the region.

Neither Venezuela nor Cuba nor Bolivia has perfected the transition to socialism – a transition that is not entirely possible in a world that remains dominated by capitalism. What they represent are experiments in socialism that are seeking, against very powerful odds, to achieve a more humane and sustainable alternative to capitalism, and as such some aspects of the processes have proven more successful than others. For instance, Bolivia is still in the formative stages, with its most profound contribution to date being proclamations related to the environment. Venezuela and Cuba, on the other hand, have implemented socialism to a much a greater degree. However, what is most important, as Lambie notes, is that, 'perhaps like never before in Latin America, there is a conscious popular upsurge among the masses that is propelling the process of change'.[30] Ultimately, what the examples of Venezuela and Cuba in particular provide us with are some valuable insights into the possibilities offered by socialism.

SOCIALISM FOR THE TWENTY-FIRST CENTURY:
VENEZUELA

Like many other nations in the global South, Venezuela implemented neoliberal reforms during the 1980s and 1990s that
contributed to an increase in the country's poverty levels. But
by the late 1990s, Venezuela's traditional parties had become
thoroughly discredited, along with the neoliberal model they
promoted. Venezuelans sought an alternative and, in December
1998, they elected Hugo Chávez to the presidency with 57 per
cent of the vote – the largest percentage total in four decades
of Venezuelan democracy. Upon assuming office, Chávez immediately set about fulfilling his campaign promise to establish
a new constitution and to ensure that all Venezuelans benefited
from the wealth generated by the country's oil production.

In 2001, the Chávez government announced the Organic Law
of Hydrocarbons, which decreed that the Venezuelan State Oil
Company (PDVSA) must hold a majority share in all joint ventures
with foreign companies so that the government, and by extension the Venezuelan people, would be the primary beneficiaries
of the country's oil wealth. Rather than continuing the wait to
see if the national wealth would eventually 'trickle down' to the
country's impoverished majority, the Chávez government instead
challenged neoliberal doctrine by using its increased oil revenues
to ensure the social well-being of the Venezuelan people, particularly the poor. The Bolivarian revolution, or 'socialism for
the twenty-first century', as the Chávez government's reforms
have been called, is intended as an alternative to neoliberalism.
At the United Nations in 2004, Chávez issued one of his many
scathing critiques of neoliberalism when he declared:

> Hunger and poverty are the most terrible of the effects of a world
> order based on neoliberal globalization. ... A world without poor and
> hungry would be achievable only through an economic and social
> order radically different from that which now prevails.[31]

According to Lisandro Pérez, a community leader in Caracas,
the Bolivarian revolution seeks to empower citizens so that

they will become passionate about social change and achieve
that radically different economic and social order. This change,
notes Pérez, cannot come from above; it must be rooted in local
communities. The objective is to create a new socialism that is
different from the centralized socialism that was so prominent
in the twentieth century. As Pérez explains,

> When the Berlin Wall fell, we thought it was the fall of socialism,
> but that wasn't true. What was the significance of the fall of the
> Berlin Wall? In reality, it was the fall of the old models, the old
> orthodoxy, and something new was rising. ... It had to fall so that a
> new political project could rise.[32]

The new political project in Venezuela seeks to avoid the
pitfalls of the failed socialist projects, or 'really existing socialism', of the twentieth century. In actuality, the Soviet Union and
the Eastern Bloc nations were neither socialist nor communist.
They constituted a form of state capitalism, because they simply
replaced one set of elites – capitalists, or economic elites – with
another one – the state, or political elites – in order to manage
an economic system that remained dedicated to capital accumulation. According to Maass,

> The state did own the means of production in the USSR. But the
> real question is: Who owns the state? If the answer is anything
> other than the mass of people, exercising their 'ownership' through
> some system of grassroots democracy – if there is an elite, however
> well- or ill-intentioned, exercising power over how society is run
> – then that's a society that violates the most basic definition of
> socialism.[33]

In the Soviet Union, the state not only owned the means of
production, it also managed it; therefore economic democracy
did not exist. There was also limited space for meaningful participation in the political sphere. Consequently, as Kovel points
out, while

> gain of state power by the revolution is essential for redirecting
> society, so must the revolution give high priority to building ways

CAPITALISM

of dissolving that power and preventing the state from turning into a monster over society. A key principle is the internal development of true democracy, the absence of which crippled all previous socialisms. That is why alternative party-building in the pre-revolutionary period is an essential – not to win state power in the here and now ... but to democratize the state insofar as possible, and to train people in the ways of self-governance so that when the revolution is made they will be in a position to sustain democratic development.[34]

Venezuela's socialist project has promoted participatory democracy in an effort to ensure that the state does not become a 'monster over society'. Nevertheless, capitalist elites and their defenders in the media frequently portray Chávez as an authoritarian leader who governs in an undemocratic manner. This is not surprising given the challenges to the interests of capital posed by the Venezuelan revolution. As political scientist Terry Gibbs notes, capitalists

are bound to find the process of wealth distribution somewhat painful and to view the policies associated with redistribution as 'authoritarian.' Interestingly, it is not said that this is the bitter medicine that the rich must swallow to see a more just and humane society. Whereas the poor, on the other hand, have been asked to swallow the bitter medicine of neo-liberal austerity for over two decades in the vain hope that some of the wealth would eventually trickle-down.[35]

For the most part, to date, the social transformation under way in Venezuela has not been authoritarian; in fact, it has been primarily rooted in participatory democracy. The central components of this participatory democracy consist of communal councils, which coordinate policies at the community level; worker-owned cooperatives; and direct democracy through national referendums. Consequently, as Naomi Klein points out,

Despite the overwhelming cult of personality surrounding Chávez, and his moves to centralise power at state level, the progressive networks in Venezuela are at the same time highly decentralised, with power dispersed at the grass roots and community level, through thousands of neighbourhood councils and co-ops.[36]

A crucial aspect of Venezuela's revolution and participatory democratic process has been the emergence of economic democracy through worker co-management of state-owned industries and the creation of more than 100,000 worker-owned co-operatives consisting of more than 1.5 million workers, who constitute 18 per cent of the nation's workforce.[37] Agricultural co-operatives have been formed in both the countryside and urban areas, alongside manufacturing co-operatives, with the principal objective being a shift of ownership of the means of production away from a minority of capitalist elites and into the hands of the broader population. As Tom Malleson explains,

> Instead of workers renting their labour to an owner in exchange for a wage, Venezuelan workers are increasingly acquiring *economic enfranchisement* – a direct say in the direction and organization of their firm, and thereby an increasing capacity to control their own lives. Hierarchy and subservience at work are being replaced, to some degree at least, with democracy and popular sovereignty.[38]

The co-operatives have emerged in conjunction with the creation of more than 16,000 communal councils that seek to empower people at the grassroots level by allowing communities to devise and implement their own development and infrastructure projects. According to Malleson,

> The councils are autonomous, though they often coordinate with municipal government, and receive funding from different government levels. Since their inauguration, the councils have been immensely successful. They are hugely popular among the citizenry, particularly in poorer areas and the *barrios* (urban neighbourhoods), and have grown dramatically in number.[39]

In addition to being vehicles for economic and participatory democracy, the co-operatives and communal councils also seek to increase national self-sufficiency through domestic production – particularly of foodstuffs – for domestic consumption.

Furthermore, in order to address gender inequities and in accordance with Article 88 of the constitution, the Venezuelan government pays women for the housework they perform in their own homes. Close to 100,000 housewives who are living in poverty receive 80 per cent of the national minimum wage in recognition that their work is an economic activity and that it contributes social welfare and social wealth to the society at large. The programme also facilitates community programmes that provide education and training to poor women as well as interest-free loans for those who wish to establish businesses.[40]

The ongoing transformation to socialism has dramatically impacted the lives of poor Venezuelans over the past decade due to the government facilitating an extensive redistribution of wealth, the delivery of free education and health care, subsidized food and housing, increased state ownership of the country's national resources, the creation of thousands of communal councils and worker-owned co-operatives, and an astounding reduction in the number of people living in poverty from 55 per cent of the population prior to Chávez's election to 26 per cent by 2008.[41] Additionally, Venezuela surpassed Chile and Costa Rica in 2008 to become the country with the second-lowest level of inequality in Latin America – the country with the lowest level being socialist Cuba.[42]

Ensuring that all citizens have free and equal access to quality health care and education has been a primary objective of the Venezuelan government's social policies. In fact, education has played a crucial role in challenging the hegemonic discourse of capital in order to stimulate a new way of thinking about society and the role of the individual. Arnaldo Sotillo, director of a school in one of the poorest neighbourhoods in Caracas, stated that the overall objective of the new education system is to emphasize 'social values and create a different citizen for the future, a better society overall'.[43]

Under neoliberalism, the underfunded public education system in Venezuela was deteriorating while enrolment in private schools of children from the middle and upper classes increased steadily. Many poor families could not afford to send their children to school and so thousands were excluded from the system. In 1998, enrolment consisted of only 59 per cent of children. Over

2 million students had dropped out before grade 6 and another 2 million had failed to complete their secondary education.[44] To address this crisis, the Chávez administration transformed the country's primary and secondary schools from traditional institutions to Bolivarian schools. The Bolivarian schools contain kitchens staffed by parents from the community who have completed an intensive state-funded nutrition course. The school kitchens provide students with breakfast, lunch and an afternoon snack in an attempt to lower the levels of malnutrition among poor Venezuelan children. The Bolivarian schools also contain computer labs, so all Venezuelan children and not only those from wealthy families have the opportunity to become computer literate in the twenty-first century. The government also launched various education programmes for illiterate adults who had failed to complete their secondary education. By 2005, almost 1.5 million previously illiterate adults had learned to write and only 2 per cent of the country's 26 million people remained illiterate, leading the government to declare Venezuela an illiteracy-free nation.[45]

Venezuela's public health system had also been ravaged by neoliberalism. It was seriously underfunded and not readily accessible to poor Venezuelans living in urban shanty towns and rural areas. For many poor Venezuelans, visiting a doctor meant travelling long distances followed by hours spent waiting in line. In 2003, in accordance with the new constitution's requirement that quality health care be freely accessible to all, the government launched Mission Barrio Adentro (Inside the Neighbourhood Mission), which was staffed with Cuban doctors. Neighbourhood health committees were formed so that citizens, particularly poor citizens, could participate in the development of health programmes rather than being passive recipients of policy. The committees are responsible for identifying their community's health needs and for contributing to the design and continuing evaluation of programmes.[46] The role of community members in taking responsibility for developing, managing and evaluating health-care projects at the neighbourhood level highlights the participatory nature of the democratic model emerging in Venezuela.

The high levels of satisfaction with the country's democratic model among Venezuelans is evident in a 2010 report issued by the region's largest polling firm, the Chile-based Corporación Latinobarómetro. As has been the case for much of the past decade, Venezuela ranked higher in virtually every category than nearly all of the other seventeen nations surveyed.[47] According to the survey, 84 per cent of Venezuelans viewed their country's democracy positively, by far the highest in the region and a significant increase over the 60 per cent who held that view the year before Chávez assumed office.[48] And with regard to the increasingly socialistic measures evident in Venezuela's economic policies, the citizens of only three countries – Uruguay, Chile and Brazil – were more satisfied with the performance of their nation's economy than were Venezuelans.[49]

Venezuela's Bolivarian revolution has not been a strictly nationalist project; Chávez has also placed great emphasis on challenging international capitalist institutions. He has done this primarily by focusing on regional integration through the Bolivarian Alternative for Latin America and the Caribbean (ALBA) as an alternative to the US-promoted free-trade model. ALBA seeks to raise the social and economic levels of the poorest nations in the region; encourage self-sufficiency in food production; pass national legislation that would favour smaller domestic business enterprises; reverse privatizations, especially of public services; and oppose intellectual property rights.[50]

An important component of ALBA has been the regional redistribution of Venezuela's oil wealth. In 2005, Chávez announced the launching of Petrocaribe, an initiative that ensures the delivery of affordable oil from Venezuela to seventeen Caribbean nations. However, Venezuela will only deal with state-owned oil companies. Under Petrocaribe, the Venezuelan state oil company, PDVSA, allows governments to utilize a barter method of payment that often includes the transfer of agricultural products or human services to Venezuela in return for oil. For instance, Venezuela exchanges 90,000 barrels of oil a day for 10,000 Cuban doctors, medical technicians, physical fitness trainers and literacy experts who staff the government's health and education missions.[51] In other words, instead of engaging in the capitalist concept of an international free-market trading system in which the principal actors are private corporations whose primary objective is the attainment of profit, Venezuela and Cuba are participating in a society-to-society barter trade process that ensures that one country receives the doctors and educators it desperately needs and the other obtains the energy supplies it frequently lacks.

Chávez has also illustrated a desire to help nations in the region reduce their dependence on international financial institutions such as the IMF and the World Bank. In July 2005, Venezuela loaned $300 million to Ecuador so that country could avoid defaulting on its foreign debt. The loan was issued when the World Bank refused to disburse a previously agreed-to $100 million loan because the IMF was not satisfied with the pace at which Ecuador was implementing neoliberal reforms.[52] And in May 2007, after finally paying off the last of the pre-Chávez-era loans, the Venezuelan president announced that Venezuela was withdrawing from the IMF and the World Bank. Six months later, Venezuela and six other South American nations – Argentina, Brazil, Bolivia, Ecuador, Paraguay and Uruguay – announced the creation of the Bank of the South. In June 2008, ministers from the seven nations agreed to provide the bank with $10 billion in initial funding.[53] The new bank, unlike the World Bank, provides unconditional development loans to governments in South America.

Venezuela is engaging in foreign policy and a trading system with its neighbours that are rooted in cooperation and solidarity rather than competition and profiteering. In essence, it is a process that reflects the argument made by Mészáros that socialism cannot be achieved in isolation; it must be a global process. Venezuela's achievements have been made possible in part by the solidarity that has emerged between nations in Latin

America, which has made it much more difficult for the United States to isolate Venezuela politically and economically in the manner it did Cuba and Nicaragua in the second half of the twentieth century.

At this point, many features of the Bolivarian revolution are more social-democratic than socialist, since the private sector continues to exist in Venezuela and the government's role has largely been to oversee a redistribution of the national wealth. But by establishing thousands of worker-owned co-operatives and implementing a participatory democracy that contrasts sharply with the liberal democratic models in North America and Europe, the socialist project in Venezuela has already shown itself to be more radical than the social-democratic reforms implemented in the global North during the Keynesian era.

Rather than applying liberal concepts of incorporating the marginalized into an existing liberal-democratic institutional framework, Venezuela has sought to restructure the political system to address education, health care and other social issues by creating projects – called missions – that are formulated, implemented and evaluated by people at the grassroots level – in other words, by the people who are most impacted by them. The missions, along with the communal councils, exist in a parallel form to the state's traditional liberal-democratic institutions and are intended to empower the country's poor. In reference to these parallel structures, Žižek explains that

> what Hugo Chávez has begun doing in Venezuela differs markedly from the standard liberal form of inclusion: Chávez is not including the excluded in a pre-existing liberal-democratic framework; he is, on the contrary, taking the 'excluded' dwellers of favelas as his *base* and then reorganizing political space and political forms of organization so that the latter will 'fit' the excluded. Pedantic and abstract as it may appear, this difference – between 'bourgeois democracy' and 'dictatorship of the proletariat' – is crucial.[54]

Venezuela's experiment in participatory democracy is an example of how, as Hayek stated, it is 'possible for a democracy to govern with a total lack of liberalism'. Ironically, the 'illiberal' democracy in Venezuela is much more reflective of 'government of the people, by the people, for the people' than the 'liberal' democracy in the United States, which prioritizes the interests of capital. This reality is evidenced by Venezuela's impressive gains in democratizing workplaces and society in general, a process that has resulted in dramatic decreases in both poverty and inequality.

SOCIALISM FOR THE TWENTY-FIRST CENTURY: CUBA

In many ways, Cuba has been an exception to the top-down 'democratic centralism' so prevalent in the 'actually existing socialism' of the twentieth century. And, as we have seen, the small island nation has played an important role in helping Venezuela address its social crisis, particularly in the areas of health and education. But Cuba's contribution to Venezuela's social transformation is not limited to health and education assistance; its experiments in participatory democracy have also influenced the formulation of socialism in Venezuela.

In the early years of the Cuban Revolution, 'Che' Guevara challenged democratic centralism by seeking to achieve a more decentralized and participatory production process. Beginning in 1962, as minister of industry, Guevara sought to shift decision-making and management of production to the factory level. However, the shift towards a participatory democracy and worker management of factories lost momentum when Guevara departed Cuba in 1964.[55] Over the next decade, many aspects of socialism in Cuba reflected the Soviet model of 'scientific socialism', although it still retained a modicum of the participatory model desired by Guevara, evident in the widespread citizen engagement in the Committees for the Defence of the Revolution (CDRs).

But in the 1970s, largely in response to economic failures caused by centralized national policymaking, the Cuban government sought to return to Guevara's concept of a more decentralized and participatory model. According to political scientist

Emilio Duharte Díaz, Cuba has since sought to reflect Marxist
revolutionary socialism more closely by creating a model that
is 'more human, more democratic and broadly participatory,
more renovating and creative, country-specific, and free from
the kind of doctrinaire, dogmatic preconceptions and other
misrepresentations that caused the collapse of Eastern Europe
and the USSR'.[56]

In order to achieve this shift, thousands of meetings between
government officials, workers and members of community organizations were held throughout the country, with the result
being the establishment in 1976 of new governing structures
called Organs of People's Power (OPP). In the ensuing years,
and particularly following further reforms in the early 1990s,
the OPP structure evolved to consist of elected assemblies at the
municipal, provincial and national levels that are responsible
for enacting legislation under the Cuban constitution of 1976.
While the Cuban Communist Party is still the official party of the
nation, it is not permitted to put forth candidates or campaign
in elections – neither are the other parties that were allowed to
form after 1992. Candidates for OPP assemblies stand for office
as individuals and not as party representatives, and more than 25
per cent of those elected at the municipal level are not members
of the Communist Party.[57]

Between two and eight individual candidates, who have been
nominated by neighbourhood assemblies, vie for each seat in
municipal elections held every two-and-a-half years. The candidates post a photograph and biography of themselves in specified
public locations and the people vote for their desired candidate
on election day. There is no campaigning and, therefore, no
funding of campaigns. Consequently, as political scientist Robert
Buddan points out, 'There is no financial competition between
campaigns in Cuba and money does not determine who wins as
it does in so many western elections.'[58]

Candidates for the National Assembly are proposed by the
elected delegates of the municipal OPPs and by hundreds of
nominating assemblies held throughout the country consisting

of members of the CDRs and organizations representing workers, youth, farmers, women and other sectors of society. For the most part, it is in the debates that take place in these nominating assemblies that the democratic process at the national level occurs. Through this process one candidate is nominated for each of the 614 seats in the National Assembly, and then each nominee must receive at least 50 per cent of the national vote in elections held every five years. If a candidate fails to obtain more than 50 per cent of the vote, then another must be nominated and stand for election. The National Assembly then elects the Council of State, which in turn elects the president.[59] Any elected official can be recalled by the electorate at any time if his or her performance is deemed unsatisfactory.

In what Buddan has called a 'bottom-up democracy', voter turnout routinely runs higher than 90 per cent, and women constitute 35 per cent of delegates elected to the National Assembly – resulting in Cuba ranking sixth out of 162 nations globally in gender equality in parliament.[60] As Lambie notes with regard to Cuba's democratic process, 'To some extent, the state can guide and manipulate this process, but if it exceeds its rights and obligations it could tip the balance and lose the asset on which its legitimacy depends: social consensus.'[61]

Unlike what so often occurs under liberal-democratic systems, participation in Cuba is not limited to casting ballots, particularly at the municipal level. Elected municipal officials hold consultative meetings every week in which citizens deliver requests and make complaints. Every six months, public meetings are held in which elected officials are required to explain how they responded to the requests and complaints. It is not unusual for as many as eighty per cent of eligible voters to attend these meetings, which stands in stark contrast to the lack of citizen participation at the municipal level in the liberal democracies of wealthy nations in the global North. As Lambie notes, 'It is at this point of contact between citizen, delegate, and in turn the government's administrative and delivery systems, that participation in Cuba's formal democracy is most visibly exercised.'[62]

One of the motivating factors in the high levels of participation is the social ownership of the means of production. In Cuba, the state accounts for approximately 90 per cent of formal economic activity, with provincial and municipal OPPs being responsible for much of it.[63] Consequently, citizen participation in weekly and bi-annual meetings – in addition to voting in elections and involvement in worker-managed co-operatives – provides people with an influential voice not only in political and social matters such as health and education, but also in economic policymaking and in the operation of their workplaces. This economic democracy contrasts sharply with municipal politics in liberal democracies under capitalism, where the means of production are privately owned, thereby closing off any space for participatory decision-making and ensuring that business owners cannot be held accountable by workers and community members. In short, and in contrast to capitalist societies, democracy in Cuba exists in both political and economic spheres.

Cuba has been labelled a dictatorship by many analysts because political parties cannot field candidates in elections and Cubans cannot vote directly for their president, as occurs in representative democracies. Critics, however, ignore the fact that democracy in Cuba transcends the political sphere and includes the economic realm, thereby allowing people a direct voice in policy decisions at the municipal level, where people's lives are most directly impacted by government. Social ownership of the means of production as part of a participatory democracy has resulted in high levels of citizen engagement and empowerment. Ultimately, then, the problem from the perspective of capital is not so much a lack of democracy in Cuba, but rather that the country is not a liberal democracy that prioritizes capital's needs.

This process of participatory democracy has resulted in Cuba's socialist system enjoying a much greater degree of legitimacy among the population than that which existed in the Soviet Union and other Eastern bloc nations – and is a major reason why socialism in Cuba has survived in the post-Cold War era. As Lambie notes in regard to Cuba,

[I]t is neither a typical authoritarian dictatorship nor a typical socialist state, at least as represented by the command economy model of the twentieth century. Instead, it presents a complex mix of nationalism and socialism that can be distinguished by significant levels of interaction between leaders and the masses, and a popular commitment to participation. The Cuban Revolution should not simply be seen either as a defunct system or a champion of a specific set of structuralist, Soviet-style socialist achievements, but can perhaps be more accurately understood as a unique political and economic process that is still in flux. Although the pull of the market is strong, the continuing influence of the island's anti-capitalist Revolution, with its emphasis on equality and participation, is still an important factor in shaping its future.[64]

Within this system, the Cuban Communist Party is not a political party in the sense of the term under liberal democracy because it is not an electoral party. It nevertheless remains highly influential in the country's political affairs because more than 7 million Cubans – out of a population of 11 million – belong to the Party. Therefore, the Communist Party represents a diverse array of views from among the population and is responsive to the wishes of its members. At its national congress in April 2011, the Party announced that it was implementing the many recommendations for internal reforms that emerged from public debates involving millions of its members.[65] In regard to the Cuban Communist Party, Lambie explains,

The Party in Cuba is seen by the population in a different light than were ruling Communist Parties in the former socialist countries. In the latter, the Party was held by many to be an institution which gave its members access to privileges unavailable to the rest of the population, was rife with corruption, insensitive to the needs of the people and in general constituted an elite political class. In Cuba, very few people regard the Party in this way, and such a perception would indeed be inaccurate. The PCC may share some of the faults of its counterparts in the former Communist countries, but to a significantly lesser degree, especially regarding corruption which is very dimly regarded by the Cuban leadership. Clearly, the role of the Party ... does not significantly suppress or render ineffectual the democratic and participatory process at local level.[66]

Nevertheless, Cuba's democratic structures do not provide space in which political opposition can publicly advocate for a transition from socialism to capitalism because such a shift would undermine the basic tenet of the revolution: equality, which is enshrined in the country's socialist constitution. Since inequality – and by extension structural violence – is inherent in capitalism, then capitalism is deemed to be incompatible with a society that seeks to achieve equality by ensuring that everyone's basic needs – food, housing, health care and education – are met in an egalitarian manner. In many ways, Cuba is attempting to ensure that it does not suffer the fate of so many sustainable indigenous societies by avoiding the conditions under which, as Kovel earlier noted, 'the virus of capital, with its promise of limitless wealth and godlike transformation, is able to take hold'. Of course, this issue would be mostly moot in a socialist world.

Similarly, in the United States there is very little space in which to espouse anti-capitalist views. The US Congress is overwhelmingly dominated by pro-capitalist Republicans and Democrats; all Supreme Court justices are appointed by the two dominant parties; alternative parties are barred from participating in election debates and have difficulty accessing funding (even public funding); and the corporate-owned mainstream media refuse to present perspectives that challenge the hegemonic discourse of capital.[67] The hegemonic structures that marginalize anti-capitalist views in the United States are much more insidious than those in Cuba, but they are nonetheless just as, if not more, effective. Furthermore, unlike in Cuba, the hegemonic structures under capitalism defend and promote a genocidal system.

Despite being a small nation with few natural resources to speak of, Cuba has succeeded in meeting the basic food and housing needs of all of its citizens and has provided free education and health-care systems that are among the best in the world. Cuba has managed for the most part to preserve these social achievements despite the loss of its largest trading partner and supplier of aid – the Soviet Union – and a corresponding intensification of the US economic embargo intended to undermine the Cuban socialist example. These factors made it particularly challenging for Cuba to meet the basic needs of its people during the 1990s, a period of adjustment known as the 'Special Period'. In a post-Cold War world dominated by neoliberal globalization, Cuba had little option but to engage with the broader global capitalist economy. But the corresponding reforms, such as opening up the country to foreign investment in areas such as tourism – albeit in joint ventures with the state – did not constitute the beginning of a transition to a market economy. As Cuba's Vice President Carlos Lage stated, 'Our opening is not an opening toward capitalism, but rather a socialist opening towards a capitalist world. It is based on certain principles that guarantee the preservation of socialist order over our economy and our ability to meet our economic and social objectives.'[68]

While the reforms implemented during the Special Period have posed challenges to the revolutionary socialist project in Cuba, they have permitted the country to preserve its impressive social gains, particularly in the areas of health and education. Cuba has one doctor for approximately every one hundred families, resulting in a ratio of physicians per 1,000 people that is twice as high as in the United States.[69] Cuba has also established internationally recognized research and development facilities in biotechnology, immunology and other areas, and has become a world leader in the production of vaccines.[70]

As a result of its emphasis on social well-being, Cuba has achieved health indicators far superior to every other nation in Latin America and comparable to those in many wealthy countries of the global North. For instance, life expectancy in Cuba is 78 years, which is one year higher than in the United States. Similarly, Cuba's infant and child mortality rates – deaths of children under 1 and under 5 years of age respectively – are both superior to those in the United States. When Cuba's health indicators are compared to capitalist nations in Latin America, the differences are astounding. Cuba's infant mortality rate of 5.6 per 1,000 births compares to 19.0 in Mexico, 24.2 in Colombia and 14.4 in relatively wealthy Argentina. A similar discrepancy exists between socialist Cuba and its capitalist neighbours in the region with regard to child mortality rates.[71] Not only do the social indicators of Latin America's capitalist nations pale in comparison to those of Cuba, but these countries also are not forced to endure an oppressive economic embargo at the hands of the United States – in fact, many of them even receive significant 'development' aid from Washington and international institutions such as the World Bank.

Despite the economic challenges Cuba faces due to the US embargo and to its relatively isolated position as an island of socialism in an ocean of capitalism, Cuba has succeeded in ensuring that the fundamental needs of all of its citizens are met. In 2007, UN Special Rapporteur Jean Ziegler visited Cuba on a fact-finding mission related to food security and declared at the end of it that he had not encountered a single malnourished person; a far cry from the reality in virtually every nation in the global South existing under capitalism.[72]

As evidenced by its role in Venezuela, Cuba's socialist health-care model is rooted in a concept of solidarity with poor and marginalized peoples throughout the world, and in Latin America and sub-Saharan Africa in particular. Such an approach is only possible under a social system that prioritizes human need over profit. For example, beginning in 1997, Cuba engaged in a medical cooperation agreement with Haiti; ten years later Cuban medical staff were caring for 75 per cent of the population. During that time, infant mortality rates per 1,000 births plunged from 80 to 33, and life expectancy increased from 54 to 61 years.[73] Similarly, in 2004, Cuba launched 'Operation Miracle' to restore eyesight to poor people throughout the global South suffering from cataracts and glaucoma. The project was initiated after Cubans engaged in literacy projects in Venezuela discovered that many poor people could not learn to read and write because of impaired eyesight. In its first five years, at no cost to the patients, the programme restored sight to more than 1.6 million people in twenty-eight nations and established eye surgery clinics throughout Latin America and Africa.[74]

Perhaps one of the most compelling examples of Cuba's international solidarity is its establishment of a medical clinic in Havana in 1990 to provide free health care to Ukranian children who had become sick from radiation poisoning – and to children born to parents contaminated with radiation – resulting from the 1986 Chernobyl nuclear disaster. Over the past twenty years, the Tarara Clinic has treated more than 18,000 Ukranian children for cancer and other radiation-related illnesses, with some of them staying at the clinic for as long as a year at a time. The Cuban government covers all the costs of room, board, medical treatment and schooling for each of the children, with medical costs alone estimated to have totalled more than $300 million.[75] The Cuban economy receives no benefits from treating these children; in fact, the Tarara Clinic constitutes a significant drain on the country's economy. Nevertheless, Cuba's socialist system continues to treat these children who cannot afford medical care back home because human well-being is prioritized over economic growth.

Ultimately, Cuba seeks to train domestic personnel in the countries in which they work so they can eventually operate their own health-care systems. To this end, the Cuban government provides scholarships annually to thousands of people from nations throughout the global South to attend Cuban medical schools, with the only stipulation being that the new doctors return home to practise medicine for a minimum of five years – rather than emigrating with their newfound skills to wealthy capitalist nations as part of the brain drain from South to North.[76] Tellingly, Cuba's number one export is health care. This contrasts dramatically with the leading export of the United States, which is weaponry.[77]

Cuba's shift towards a more participatory democratic model over the past few decades, along with its emphasis on equality and human need rather than profits and economic growth, has influenced the socialism for the twenty-first century that is emerging in Latin America, particularly in Venezuela. And despite facing huge obstacles, including having to learn how to coexist with a global capitalist economy and related market pressures, Cuba's socialist experiment continues to avoid the worst of the social maladies that plague so many capitalist nations in the global South. As Lambie explains,

> It cannot be denied that Cuba's massive economic contraction, after the collapse of the Soviet bloc, and now the effects of global recession, have left sections of society in poverty and with limited work opportunities. Inevitably, under such circumstances, social breakdown and decay have taken place. However, a similar account could be written about the poor quarters in virtually any Third World city. But the difference is that in Havana, and Cuba generally, even the most wretched members of society have access to health care, education, and basic sustenance. They also have relative freedom from the horrors of gang warfare that have taken over many cities in Latin America and the Caribbean ... One should further consider the systematic state violence that still exists in many countries in the region, whereas the Cuban state, despite its problems, is benign towards the population, and its objective remains to provide a reasonable existence for all.[78]

In response to the challenges mentioned by Lambie, there has been an ongoing debate in Cuba regarding the degree to which the country's reforms should facilitate a 'socialist opening towards a capitalist world' and the direction that the revolution should take in the twenty-first century. Public consultations have shown that there is broad popular support for defending the social gains achieved over the past few decades, which requires the continued prioritization of social and economic rights. The emphasis on these collective rights has made Cuba a focal point in the battle over the hegemonic discourse related to human rights. The dominant human rights paradigm as manifested in NGOs such as Amnesty International and Human Rights Watch has helped to defend the interests of capital through its prioritization of individual rights over collective rights. Consequently, Cuba has been vilified, particularly by the United States, for violations of certain human rights.

The dominant human rights model under capitalism prioritizes individual rights – particularly the right to private property – to the degree that they cannot be significantly infringed upon in order to ensure that the collective – social and economic – rights of everyone in the community are protected. This is why there is no right to food, housing or health care for citizens of the United States, where some 18,000 people die annually due to a lack of access to medical treatment.[79] Consequently, the social and economic rights of millions of people are violated in order to defend individual rights, and this is viewed as perfectly legitimate under the hegemonic discourse and logic of capital. But when a country such as Cuba defends the collective rights of all of its citizens with regard to access to food, housing, education and health care against the threats posed by those who seek to prioritize individual rights in a manner that violates the country's socialist constitution, then the Cuban government is portrayed as a major violator of human rights.

Clearly, it is crucial that collective rights be defended through a participatory democratic process rather than through authoritarian dictates in order to avoid the atrocities that occurred under Pol Pot and Stalin. Ultimately, participatory democracy is essential in order to avert the mass human suffering, even genocide, that will likely result from the prioritization of collective rights under an authoritarian 'communist' regime or the prioritization of individual rights under the capitalist system.

In order to defend the collective rights of Cubans, the Cuban government has imprisoned dissidents for their opposition to the revolution. It claims that many of the political prisoners in its jails are Cubans who have received funding from a foreign government that is intent on achieving regime change. One such foreign programme has been conducted by the US Agency for International Development (USAID), which, under the guise of 'democracy promotion', distributes Internet and satellite communications equipment to certain Cuban groups in direct violation of Cuban law. The project came to light when US aid worker Alan Gross, under contract to USAID, was arrested by the Cuban government in 2009.[80] This case constitutes the latest example of the constant threat posed to the socialist system in Cuba by the world's most powerful capitalist nation, which is actively engaged in a campaign to destroy the revolution through its continuation of an inhumane economic embargo and other actions.

Interestingly, the number of detentions in Cuba pales in comparison to the scale of human rights abuses perpetrated in recent decades by capitalist regimes in Colombia, Haiti, Guatemala, El Salvador, Chile, Argentina and other countries throughout the region. According to international human rights groups, the principal human rights violation in Cuba is the imprisonment of 'dissidents' by the government. Amnesty International lists fifty-five 'prisoners of conscience' in Cuba, while the Cuban Commission for Human Rights and National Reconciliation claims there are 167 political prisoners on the island.[81] In sharp contrast, there are more than 7,500 political prisoners currently incarcerated in Colombia, which has been the neoliberal poster child in Latin America for the past decade.[82] The objective here is not to justify the human rights violations perpetrated by the Cuban state but to use this discrepancy to highlight how the hegemonic discourse of capital has successfully kept the human rights spotlight disproportionately focused on Cuba while simultaneously distracting people's attention away from the country's impressive social gains achieved through its defence of social and economic rights.

Cuba illustrates the difficulty – or impossibility – of implementing socialism in one country. On the one hand, reforms that downsize the public sector and provide licences for small businesses threaten to undermine the socialist project and illustrate the challenges faced by a small isolated socialist nation that is forced not only to engage with a capitalist world, but to engage with it under the constraints of an oppressive economic embargo. On the other hand, the emergence of the socialist project in Venezuela along with other left-leaning governments in Latin America has diminished the degree of isolation that Cuba experienced during the 1990s and may ultimately provide greater opportunities for preserving and even furthering the country's social achievements.

In the meantime, Cuba's socialist experiment continues to try to create a society marked by human development rather than the consumerism and alienation inherent in a market economy dominated by a culture of individualism. As Fidel Castro made clear in 2005, Cuba 'will never be a society of consumption ... It will be a society of knowledge, of culture, of the most extraordinary human development that one can imagine.'[83] While Cuba has not yet fully achieved such an exalted state, its socialist system has addressed the plight of the marginalized throughout the global South far more effectively than has capitalism.

ECOSOCIALISM FOR THE TWENTY-FIRST CENTURY

One of the major issues that any new socialist project must address is the ecological crisis caused by capital. As Bolivia's President Evo Morales stated,

> Competition and the thirst for profit without limits of the capitalist system are destroying the planet. Under capitalism we are not human beings but consumers. Under capitalism Mother Earth does not exist, instead there are raw materials. Capitalism is the source of the asymmetries and imbalances in the world.[84]

Therefore ecological sustainability must be at the core of any new socialist project. A failure to address the ecological crisis will render the revolutionary project irrelevant since it will replicate one of the principal shortcomings of the industrial socialism prevalent in the twentieth century in countries such as the Soviet Union. As Kovel warns,

> Despite all the recognition of the fact that there is a global crisis of nature for which capital is primarily responsible, the fact remains that minding nature still tends to strike the typical socialist as an afterthought, both in the sense that nature does not come immediately to the socialist mind, as well as that the caring for nature is something added onto existing socialist doctrine rather than integral to it. ... Therefore, unless the socialist revolution also undoes the domination of nature, which is to say, becomes ecosocialist,

its satisfactions – and the needs and use-values in which they are grounded – are going to tend to reproduce the past.[85]

Ecosocialism, according to Kovel, is a 'society in which production is carried out by freely associated labor and with consciously ecocentric means and ends'.[86] Similarly, Ian Angus explains,

> Ecosocialism has grown out of two parallel political trends – the spread of Marxist ideas in the green movement and the spread of ecological ideas in the Marxist left. The result is a set of social and political goals, a growing body of ideas, and a global movement. Ecosocialism's goal is to replace capitalism with a society in which common ownership of the means of production has replaced capitalist ownership, and in which the preservation and restoration of ecosystems will be central to all activity.[87]

The ecosocialist approach is evident in the transformation to socialism under way in Latin America. Bolivia's President Morales and his ruling Movement Towards Socialism (MAS) party have sought to address the ecological crisis through legislation that reflects traditional indigenous values. As part of its implementation of 'communitarian socialism', the Bolivian government has proposed a 'Law of Mother Earth', which requires that human society live in harmony with the earth and that the earth has the right to maintain the integrity of its ecosystems through the preservation of clean air and water, and the maintenance of diversity and equilibrium. As Bolivia's foreign minister David Choquehuanca declared,

> In Bolivia we seek a return to balance, a harmonious life not only between individuals but between man and nature, so today must be a day of reflection of awareness of all to care for our Mother Earth and take timely means for our mother back to its natural balance.[88]

As part of this process, Bolivia is seeking to move towards greater food self-sufficiency by promoting the local and sustainable production of high-quality food crops. The government has committed $500 million annually over the next ten years in order to achieve this goal. This funding will be used to promote small-scale farming and to gain ownership of seeds in order to liberate farmers from the patents held by seed corporations. Carlos Romero, minister of rural development and agriculture, explains that seed ownership is crucial to the food revolution under way in Bolivia because seeds 'are a major factor in food production. But in recent years we've seen an increase in their price across the world, because of a rise in oil prices and the monopoly exercised on seeds by a few corporations. That's why we want to create state-owned companies that produce seeds.'[89]

Ecological sustainability has also become a primary policy objective of Cuba's socialist government. Over the past fifteen years, Cuba has developed into an ecosocialist nation by becoming the world's leader in organic agriculture. The collapse of its leading trading partner, the Soviet Union, and a corresponding tightening of the US economic embargo, forced Cuba to devise new ways to feed its population during the 1990s. According to Cuban permaculturalist Roberto Pérez, the country established the foundation for a more sustainable society more than fifty years ago:

> when the revolution gained sovereignty over the resources of the country, especially the land and the minerals, this was the base for sustainability. You cannot think about sustainability if your resources are in the hands of a foreign country or in private hands. Even without knowing, we were creating the basis for sustainability.[90]

By the end of the 1990s, Cuba had implemented a dramatic shift away from industrial agricultural practices reliant on fossil fuels towards sustainable organic practices – an approach that Venezuela is currently emulating. An astounding 86 per cent of Cuba's domestic agricultural production is organic and the country has also become a leader in urban agriculture, which reduces the environmental costs related to transporting food from where it is produced to those who consume it.[91] As a result of the explosion in urban agriculture, ecologist David Tracey notes, 'Today, there are kiosks all over [Havana] selling fresh food that was picked less than four hours ago.'[92] The break-up of large

state-owned farms into smaller worker-managed co-operatives
and the development of urban agriculture constitute significant
components of this new agricultural model that Lambie has called
'the largest conversion from conventional agriculture to organic
and semi-organic farming that the world has ever known'.[93]

As a result of this conversion, Cuba has reduced its use of
chemical pesticides from 21,000 tonnes a day to just 1,000.
Meanwhile, more than 50 per cent of the vegetables consumed
by Havana's 2.2 million inhabitants are now supplied by urban
agriculture; that number increases to between 80 and 100 per
cent for smaller towns and villages throughout the country. This
shift to small-scale organic agriculture has also been an economic
driver, having created more than 140,000 jobs by 2006.[94]

Based on the country's social indicators and its ecological practices, the World Wildlife Fund's *Living Planet Report* declared in
2006 that Cuba was the only nation in the world to have achieved
sustainable development.[95] Meanwhile, the same WWF report
noted that four Planet Earths would be required for everyone
in the world to live in the same manner as people in the United
States.[96] The reason for Cuba's success, Pérez suggests, is that
'sustainable development is only possible when you have social
justice'.[97] Furthermore, Cuba's scientific achievements in the field
of medicine and its successes with sustainable organic agriculture
dispel the myth that innovation is unique to capitalism.

The ecological focus of the socialist experiments emerging
in Latin America in the early twenty-first century differentiates
them from the industrial societies that dominated the 'actually
existing socialism' of the twentieth century. But ecosocialist
approaches are not unique to Latin America; they are becoming increasingly prevalent at the community level throughout
the world. But while they constitute inspirational examples of
ecocentric production, they have yet to pose any serious threat
to capital. As Kovel argues,

> For as they now exist, instances of ecocentric production are both
> scattered and mainly entrapped like irritants in the pores of capital.

The task is to free them and connect them, so that their inherent potential may be realized. We cannot rest until ecocentric production has become an ecocentric *mode* of production.[98]

CONCLUSION

Despite their impressive achievements, Venezuela and Cuba still face formidable challenges. For instance, while the hegemony of capital has been challenged in Venezuela, it nevertheless still plays a prominent role in the country. Also, Venezuela's incremental shift to socialism will require that the country address serious ecological issues related to its hyper-dependence on oil production and global markets to fund its socialist transition. Furthermore, Venezuela must address high crime rates that, despite significant achievements in reducing poverty and inequality, are largely related to the reality that one in four Venezuelans remain impoverished. Ultimately, if Venezuela is to achieve a more democratic, egalitarian and sustainable society, it must overcome the continued dominance of capital and the remaining private ownership of the means of production. A failure to implement economic democracy fully throughout the country will inevitably leave the revolution vulnerable. Meanwhile, the participatory democracy that has emerged in Cuba over the past few decades, while facilitating extensive citizen input into policymaking at the local level, could nevertheless be deepened with regard to politics at the national level. And while Cuba is still the most equal nation in Latin America, the country must contend with increases in inequality that have resulted from its engagement with the capitalist world since the end of the Cold War.

Perhaps most importantly, Venezuela, Cuba and other nations engaged in a transformation to socialism need to ensure that they do not regress to the top-down practices so prevalent in the 'actually existing socialism' of the last century and in liberal-democratic models. As Venezuelan sociologist Edgardo Lander warns, 'The worst that could happen in Venezuela would be a situation where we are confronted with two options: Stalinism or neoliberalism. If that happens, we would be in a serious mess.'[99]

In many ways, the transformation to socialism under way in Latin America, with its emphasis on the emancipation of both people and nature, more closely reflects the emancipatory vision of Marx than did the 'actually existing socialism', or Stalinism, of the twentieth century. At its core, socialism is a social system that is organized democratically and that prioritizes production for use-value over production for exchange-value. In other words, it prioritizes human need over profit. In fact, exchange-value is effectively eliminated from the equation, thereby drastically diminishing the potential for ecologically destructive production since the profit-motive has been removed.

The emphasis on social ownership of the means of production and the establishment of participatory democracy are emancipating millions of people in Latin America. However, socialism cannot focus solely on the emancipation of people in order to end the structural genocide that is capitalism. If socialism is to avoid perpetrating structural genocide against future generations, then ecologically sustainable development must be an integral part of the system. As Marx noted,

> From the standpoint of a higher economic form of society, private ownership of the globe by single individuals will appear quite as absurd as private ownership of one man by another. Even a whole society, a nation, or even all simultaneously existing societies taken together, are not the owners of the globe. They are only its possessors, its usufructuaries, and, like *boni patres familias*, they must hand it down to succeeding generations in an improved condition.[100]

CONCLUSION

You cannot make a socialist revolution without really trying.

Ernest Mandel

While more than 10 million people die annually as a result of capitalism's structural genocide, hundreds of millions more suffer non-fatal forms of structural violence such as trying to survive on a non-living wage or no wage at all, a lack of basic housing, hunger, sickness and many other social injustices. Furthermore, the structural violence perpetrated against these people often results in them also being victimized by direct physical violence in the forms of criminal aggression, state repression, social cleansing and even suicide. At the core of this structural genocide is an inequality in power and wealth that ensures the interests of capital are prioritized over those of the majority of human beings and of nature.

Samir Amin believes that it is perfectly viable for capital to continue with its expansion through accumulation by dispossession and ultimately displace the world's remaining 3 billion peasants – in fact, its internal logic requires it to do so. But what will happen to these 3 billion peasants? Amin points out that even if completely unrealistic global annual economic growth levels of 7 per cent could be achieved for the next fifty years, it would not be sufficient to meet the needs of one-third of this huge pool of surplus labourers. Therefore, he argues,

> Capitalism, by its nature, cannot resolve the peasant question: the only prospects it can offer are a planet full of slums and billions of 'too many' human beings.... I thus conclude that capitalism has entered into its phase of declining senility: the logic of the system is no longer able to ensure the simple survival of humanity. Capitalism is becoming barbaric and leads directly to genocide.[1]

But while Amin speaks of capitalism becoming genocidal in the future, it is evident from the case studies explored here that more than 10 million people are already dying annually as a result of capitalism's structural genocide. After all, capital has always addressed, as Amin puts it, 'the peasant question' through structural violence and structural genocide, evident in its annihilation of the indigenous peoples in the Americas, its forced displacement of millions of Africans from their lands to become slaves in the Americas, the dispossession of land from peasants in Britain and other Western European nations through Enclosure Acts, and the expulsion of the peasantry throughout the global South under neoliberal globalization. And, given that half of the world's population still relies on agriculture for its survival, the structural genocide is likely to continue well into the future, particularly in light of the fact that the labour of these dispossessed peasants is not required for producing goods and they are too poor to be consumers, thereby rendering them disposable. Which begs the question posed by Amin: 'If capitalism has got to the point that it considers half of humanity a "superfluous population", might it not be that capitalism itself has now become a mode of social organisation that is superfluous?'[2]

Ultimately, in order to address these social injustices, capital must be displaced from its current hegemonic position by whatever means are available. Anything less will result in a continuation of the structural genocide and the related ecological crisis. Here it is important to note that all previous social systems throughout human history either imploded or were forcibly replaced at some point. Similarly, as Mészáros notes,

The fraudulence and domination of capital and the exploitation of the working class cannot go on forever. The producers cannot be kept constantly and forever under control. Marx argued that capitalists are simply the personifications of capital. They are not free agents; they are executing the imperatives of this system. So the problem for humanity is not simply to sweep away one bunch of capitalists. To simply put one type of personification of capital in the place of another would lead to the same disaster, and sooner or later we'd end up with the restoration of capitalism.[3]

Therefore it is essential that a revolutionary transformation be systemic and that it ensure capital not return to the hegemonic position it currently enjoys. At stake are the lives of billions of people who are destined to become victims of the ongoing structural genocide. Under the logic of capital, notes Amin, the continuation of accumulation by dispossession and 'the destruction of the peasant reserves of cheap labour at the world level will result in nothing less than the genocide of half of humanity'.[4]

There is, however, no guarantee that a socialist society will emerge following the implosion of capitalism. Human civilization might simply devolve into barbarism, a sort of post-apocalyptic society in which violence is rampant and our existence is reduced to the survival of the fittest – meaning the most violent – individuals and groups. In fact, before we devolve into barbarism, we might first pass through fascism as capital struggles desperately to preserve its hegemonic position and to combat its own internal contradictions. According to Kovel,

> With whatever admixture of ideologies, fascism is a potential breakdown pattern of capitalism. To say, 'it can't happen here,' is to misread the explosive tensions built into the capitalist system. All it takes is a certain degree of crisis, and fascism may be imposed, as a revolution from above, to install an authoritarian regime in order to preserve the main workings of the system.[5]

Furthermore, capitalism does not maintain a monopoly on structural genocide, as evidenced by the 'communist' projects implemented by Stalin, Pol Pot and others. However, I would argue that the structural genocide that occurred in these cases resulted from flawed attempts to implement socialism, and that socialism is not inherently genocidal. After all, the logic of socialism prioritizes social control over society and the elimination of inequality and injustice. Therefore a social system that adheres to the logic of socialism cannot result in structural violence, since the policies implemented are intended to re-distribute wealth and power. In contrast, the logic of capital requires the prioritization of wealth accumulation for a minority of the population (i.e. capitalists) – rather than the establishment of a free-market model – and, as previously argued, inequality and injustice are inevitable outcomes of actions that adhere to this logic. In other words, any structural violence and genocide that occur under socialism result from the flawed implementation of the system rather than from its internal logic.

Revolutionary transformation to a democratic, egalitarian and sustainable socialist society requires conscious organizing prior to the implosion of capitalism if it is to have any hope of succeeding. Furthermore, as Marx stated,

> Revolution is necessary ... not only because the ruling class cannot be overthrown in any other way, but also because the class overthrowing it can only in a revolution succeed in ridding itself of all the muck of ages and become fitted to found society anew.[6]

But how might such a revolution occur? Basically, there are three phases in the process. First there is the pre-revolutionary stage, during which the movement grows and works to delegitimize the existing social system. Next comes the revolutionary 'moment' in which state power is seized, most likely utilizing some degree of violence. The third and final stage is the actual revolution, which involves the social transformation of society and will likely take an extended period of time.[7]

In order to achieve such a revolution, people must first emancipate themselves from the hegemonic discourse of capital. Gramsci argues that a counter-hegemonic discourse must be formulated that will eventually replace the existing one. This process is essential because a socialist society consists of a different set of values and a different consciousness than those that exist under capitalism. However, the principal problem, as Amin notes, is that the demand for socialist concepts such as participatory democracy is not widespread because people are 'victims both of the ideological alienations specific to capitalism and of the immediate challenges of living (or even of surviving). They are not necessarily convinced that anything other than a daily adjustment and manoeuvre is possible.'[8] In other words, most people in the global North seek to consume ever-increasing amounts of material goods in their futile struggle to alleviate their alienated condition, while many people in the global South are too busy struggling to survive to be able to focus on achieving a viable alternative social system. Ultimately, though, as Robert McChesney notes,

> If people act like it is impossible to replace capitalism with something better, they all but guarantee it will be impossible to replace capitalism with something better. Demoralization and depoliticization are the necessary conditions for a 'healthy' neoliberal society.[9]

The solution, according to Amin, resides in the combining of theory and practice, or what in Marxist terms has been called revolutionary praxis – the practical application of theory, which itself is rooted in material reality.[10] In this way, the process of challenging the hegemonic discourse of capital can begin at the grassroots level under capitalism in order to lay the groundwork for a future transition to a socialist society. In many ways, because of the dominance of the hegemonic discourse of capital, this first stage poses the greatest challenge to those seeking a revolutionary transformation. It requires that people lay the foundation for change by working tirelessly to create awareness at the grassroots level of the realities of global capitalism and of the need for a socialist alternative. Eventually, the revolutionary moment will arrive – at different times in different places – when a critical mass of the population realizes that change is essential – even inevitable. In all likelihood, as previously mentioned, people in the wealthy nations of the global North will be the last to arrive at the revolutionary moment. In fact, a revolutionary transformation will likely only occur in the global North after peoples in the global South have gained sovereignty over their lives, labour, territories and resources, which will inevitably – and negatively – impact the quality of life of people in the North. At this point, a sufficient portion of the population in the global North will hopefully begin seriously questioning the viability of capitalism and seek alternatives.

The struggle to replace the hegemonic discourse of capital with one that is socialist-oriented will not end with the arrival of the revolutionary moment. The values of capital have been so deeply internalized by so many people that this process will need to continue indefinitely. Ernesto 'Che' Guevara described the challenges related to this shift away from the hegemonic discourse of capital:

> The process is two-sided. On the one hand, society acts through direct and indirect education; on the other, the individual submits to a conscious process of self-education. ... The new society in formation has to compete fiercely with the past. This past makes itself felt not only in one's consciousness – in which the residue of an education systematically oriented toward isolating the individual still weighs heavily – but also through the very character of this transition period in which commodity relations still persist. The commodity is the economic cell of capitalist society. So long as it exists its effects will make themselves felt in the organization of production and, consequently, in consciousness.[11]

Through a deeper, conscious participation in all aspects of decision-making under socialism, argues Guevara, people will begin to reach 'total consciousness as a social being, which is equivalent to the full realization as a human creature, once the chains of alienation are broken'.[12] At this point, human beings cease to be commodities valued solely for the labour they are forced to sell in order to survive and instead begin seeing themselves as active participants in a social project. However, as Guevara warns,

> The change in consciousness does not take place automatically ... there are periods of acceleration, periods that are slower, and

even retrogression. ... This transition is taking place in the midst of violent class struggles, and with elements of capitalism within it that obscure a complete understanding of its essence.[13]

Every stage of the revolutionary transformation will inevitably be portrayed by the hegemonic discourse of capital as a threat to 'our way of life' – which translates to a threat to 'the interests of capital'. Throughout history capital has responded to such threats by creating 'red scares', portraying groups or individuals seeking radical change as threats to 'national security' or, in today's parlance, labelling them as 'terrorists'. Capitalists then inevitably restrict the very same individual rights that they laud as being inviolable, as evidenced in the US government's deportations of suspected communists and anarchists in the early twentieth century, the McCarthy witch-hunt during the 1950s, and the passing of the US Patriot Act following the 9/11 attacks.

The hegemonic discourse of capital also seeks to demonize revolutionaries by portraying them as the instigators of violence – often even when they do not engage in acts of violence. In reality, those oppressed by the existing social order are not initiating violence, but merely responding to both the direct physical violence and the structural violence inherent in the capitalist system. As Paulo Freire notes,

> With the establishment of a relationship of oppression, violence has *already* begun. Never in history has violence been initiated by the oppressed. How could they be the initiators, if they themselves are the result of violence? How could they be the sponsors of something whose objective inauguration called forth their existence as oppressed? There would be no oppressed had there been no prior situation of violence to establish their subjugation. Violence is initiated by those who oppress, who exploit, who fail to recognise others as persons – not by those who are oppressed, exploited and unrecognised.[14]

Clearly, at the beginning of the twenty-first century, all the nations of the global North and most in the global South remain in the pre-revolutionary phase. But the fact that several nations in Latin America have moved to the second and third stages of a revolutionary transformation to socialism should provide inspiration to the growing numbers of people around the world who are becoming increasingly frustrated with the existing social order. And, notes Lambie,

> Unlike the formal proletariat of the 'structuralist' period of development, the new 'informal proletariat' has no party and only appeals to traditional power structures if they commit to serving its interests. The catalyst of this change is neo-liberal globalisation. The popular movement is becoming a 'class in itself' and moving in the direction of a 'class for itself': a collective agent that changes history rather than simply being a victim of the historical process.[15]

There are significant obstacles that this 'class for itself' must overcome in the process of revolutionary transformation. As Mészáros points out,

> Naturally, it would be an illusion to expect a linear ascending development in this regard. We must soberly face the fact that the adversaries of socialism have enormous resources at their disposal for protecting capital's deeply entrenched power. ... For these reasons, real setbacks and even major relapses cannot be excluded, no matter how great the need for positive solutions and how promising the initial achievements.[16]

Regardless, we have no choice but to begin laying the foundation for a social revolution. After all, it is not only the peasantry and informal sector workers in the global South who are victims of capitalism's structural genocide, but also the traditional industrial proletariat from China to Angola to Chile. Whether it is miners or child labourers or those struggling to organize workers, the violent structures of capitalism have also wrought havoc on the formal-sector workforce. Furthermore, while many indigenous peoples, people of colour, immigrants and women in the global North have suffered social injustices under capitalism, increasing numbers of those sectors in wealthy nations who have benefited from the global capitalist system will become victims of the structural violence and structural genocide due to the implementation of neoliberal policies that have undermined social programmes and contributed to growing inequality, declining real wages and unsustainable levels of personal debt. As a result, there are signs of growing discontent in the wealthy nations of the global North. Using the Arab Spring as its example, the Occupy Wall Street movement emerged in 2011 and represented the first serious indication that mainstream sectors of US society are becoming disenchanted with the status quo. While this clearly constitutes a challenge to the dominant hegemonic discourse of capital, it remains to be seen whether or not it represents the beginning of a serious threat to the structures of capitalism.

The future no longer simply consists of 'socialism or barbarism', as Rosa Luxemburg famously suggested a century ago. We are now facing a third possibility: the annihilation of the human race and the destruction of Planet Earth, which would constitute the ultimate genocidal act perpetrated by capital. Therefore our choice now consists of socialism, barbarism or extermination. Ultimately, it is up to people across the globe to make this choice. And increasing numbers are already engaging in the struggle to emancipate themselves from the authoritarian rule of capital in an effort to bring an end to capitalism's class-based structural genocide. Therefore, I conclude with the words of Slavoj Žižek, who observes that

> people willing to put their lives on the line to protest against capitalist injustice are emerging everywhere, from the US to India, China and Japan, from Latin America to Africa, the Middle East to Western and Eastern Europe. They are disparate and speak different languages, but they are not as few as may appear – and the greatest fear of the rulers is that these voices will start to reverberate and reinforce each other in solidarity. Aware that the odds are pulling us towards catastrophe, these actors are ready to act against all odds. Disappointed by twentieth-century Communism, they are ready to 'begin from the beginning' and reinvent it on a new basis. Decried by enemies as dangerous utopians, they are the only people who have really awakened from the utopian dream which holds most of us under its sway. They ... are our only hope.[17]

NOTES

INTRODUCTION

1. Sergey P. Kapitza, 'Global Population Blow-up and After: The Demographic Revolution and Sustainable Development', *Bulletin of the Georgian National Academy of Sciences*, vol. 3, no. 1, 2009, p. 9.
2. Suzana Sawyer, *Crude Chronicles: Indigenous Politics, Multinational Oil, and Neoliberalism in Ecuador* (Durham, NC: Duke University Press, 2004), p. 101.
3. Kristi Jacques, 'Environmental Justice Case Study: Texaco's Oil Production in the Ecuadorian Rainforest', University of Michigan, 2000.
4. P. Sainath, '17,368 Farm Suicides in 2009', *The Hindu*, 27 December 2010.
5. United Nations, 'Global Health Observatory Data Repository', World Health Organization, 2008.

CHAPTER 1

1. Kathleen Ho, 'Structural Violence as a Human Rights Violation', *Essex Human Rights Review*, vol. 4, no. 2, 2007, p. 3.
2. David Roberts, *Human Insecurity: Global Structures of Violence* (London: Zed Books, 2008), p. 19.
3. Paul Farmer, 'An Anthropology of Structural Violence', *Current Anthropology*, vol. 45, no. 3, 2004, p. 305.
4. Johan Galtung, 'Violence, Peace, and Peace Research', *Journal of Peace Research*, vol. 6, no. 3, 1969, p. 168.
5. Paul Farmer, *Infections and Inequalities: The Modern Plagues* (Berkeley: University of California Press, 2001), p. 79.
6. Paulo Friere, *Pedagogy of the Oppressed* (New York: Continuum, 2000), p. 55.

7. Galtung, 'Violence, Peace, and Peace Research', p. 171.
8. Office of the High Commissioner for Human Rights, 'Convention on the Prevention and Punishment of the Crime of Genocide', United Nations, 12 January 1951.
9. Beth van Schaack, 'The Crime of Political Genocide: Repairing the Genocide Convention's Blind Spot', *Yale Law Journal*, vol. 106, no. 7, 1997, p. 2265.
10. UN Secretariat, 'First Draft of the Genocide Convention', United Nations, May 1947.
11. Van Schaack, 'The Crime of Political Genocide, p. 2265.
12. Gavan McCormack, 'Reflections on Modern Japanese History in the Context of the Concept of Genocide', in Robert Gellately and Ben Kiernan (eds), *The Specter of Genocide: Mass Murder in Historical Perspective* (Cambridge: Cambridge University Press, 2003), p. 267.
13. Van Schaack, 'The Crime of Political Genocide, p. 2268.
14. Ervin Staub, *The Roots of Evil: The Origins of Genocide and Other Group Violence* (Cambridge: Cambridge University Press, 2002), p. 8.
15. Ibid.
16. Van Schaack, 'The Crime of Political Genocide, pp. 2283-4.
17. William A. Schabas, 'Genocide Law in a Time of Transition: Recent Developments in the Law of Genocide', *Rutgers Law Review*, vol. 61, no. 1, 2008, p. 162.
18. Ibid., p. 191.
19. 'Rome Statute of the International Criminal Court', United Nations, 12 July 1999.
20. Ibid.
21. Hannibal Travis, *Genocide in the Middle East: The Ottoman Empire, Iraq, and Sudan* (Durham, NC: Carolina Academic Press, 2010), p. 433.
22. Ben Kiernan, 'Letting Sudan Get Away with Murder', Yale Global Online, 4 February 2005.
23. Justice Alito, Opinion of the Court, 'Global-Tech Appliances, Inc., *Petitioners* v. *Seb S.A.* (No. 10 – 6) 594 F. 3d 1360, affirmed', Supreme Court of the United States, 31 May 2011.
24. 'Case File/Dossier No. 001/18-07-2007/ECCC/TC', Extraordinary Chambers in the Courts of Cambodia, 26 July 2010.
25. Ibid.
26. Nafeez Mosaddeq Ahmed, 'Structural Violence as a Form of Genocide: The Impact of the International Economic Order', *Entelequia: Revista Interdisciplinar* 5, 2007, p. 4.
27. Joel Kovel, *The Enemy of Nature: The End of Capitalism or the End of the World?* (London: Zed Books, 2007), p. 83.
28. My use of the word 'workers' refers to all people who sell their labour for a wage and all of those who engage in non-wage labour (i.e. housework, child-rearing, subsistence agriculture, informal sector work, etc.) in the industrial, service and agricultural sectors. This definition is influenced by Marx's later writings in which he believed that traditional, non-capitalist societies in the global South could not only move directly to socialism without passing through the capitalist stage of development, but that they could also serve as a catalyst for the international revolution. Therefore my

definition of 'workers' moves beyond the industrial proletariat to include all of those non-capitalists whose way of life is threatened by capital.

29. Michael Mann, *The Dark Side of Democracy: Explaining Ethnic Cleansing* (Cambridge: Cambridge University Press, 2005), p. 17.

30. This does not mean that individuals should not be held accountable when they are clearly responsible for implementing policies that cause mass death, but rather that simply holding individuals accountable will not ultimately resolve a social problem that is rooted in the logic of a particular social system.

CHAPTER 2

1. Ludwig von Mises, *Human Action: A Treatise on Economics* (San Francisco: Fox & Wilkes, 1996), pp. 257-8.

2. Karl Polanyi, *The Great Transformation: The Political and Economic Origins of Our Time* (Boston, MA: Beacon Press, 2001), p. 46.

3. Von Mises, *Human Action*, p. 264.

4. Karl Marx, *Capital: A Critique of Political Economy*, Volume 1 (London: Penguin, 1992), p. 711.

5. Joel Kovel, *The Enemy of Nature: The End of Capitalism or the End of the World?* (London: Zed Books, 2007), p. 51.

6. John Bellamy Foster, 'A Failed System: The World Crisis of Capitalist Globalization and its Impact on China', *Monthly Review*, vol. 60, no. 10, 2009.

7. Jim Stanford, *Economics for Everyone: A Short Guide to the Economics of Capitalism* (Halifax, NS: Fernwood, 2008), p. 209.

8. Milton Friedman, *Capitalism and Freedom* (Chicago: University of Chicago Press, 2002), p. 2.

9. Ibid., p. 4.

10. Renée Salas, 'Friedrich von Hayek, Leader and Master of Liberalism', *El Mercurio*, 12 April 1981.

11. Ludwig von Mises, 'The Causes of the Economic Crisis: An Address', in Percy L. Greaves, Jr. (ed.), *The Causes of the Economic Crisis, and Other Essays Before and After the Great Depression* (Auburn, AL: Ludwig von Mises Institute, 2006), p. 158.

12. Ibid.

13. Robert W. McChesney, 'Introduction', in Noam Chomsky, *Profit Over People: Neoliberalism and Global Order* (New York: Seven Stories Press, 1998), p. 9.

14. Stanford, *Economics for Everyone*, p. 234.

15. Polanyi, *The Great Transformation*, p. 60.

16. Friedrich A. Hayek, 'The Moral Element in Free Enterprise', *The Freeman: Ideas on Liberty*, vol. 12, no. 7, 1962.

17. Samir Amin, *Ending the Crisis of Capitalism or Ending Capitalism?* (Cape Town: Pambazuka Press, 2011), p. 180.

18. Mark Weisbrot, 'U.S. Trade Policy: "Do As We Say, Not As We Did"', *Counterpunch*, 14 June 2002.

19. Ernesto 'Che' Guevara, 'Socialism and the Man in Cuba', in David Deutschmann (ed.), *Che Guevara Reader: Writings on Politics and Revolution* (Melbourne: Ocean Press, 2003), p. 215.

20. Von Mises, *Human Action*, pp. 592-3.
21. Karl Marx and Friedrich Engels, *The Communist Manifesto* (New York: Bantam Books, 1992), pp. 20-21.
22. Karl Marx, *Grundrisse: Foundations of the Critique of Political Economy* (London: Penguin, 1993), p. 407.
23. István Mészáros, *The Structural Crisis of Capital* (New York: Monthly Review Press, 2010), p. 109.
24. David Harvey, *The New Imperialism* (Oxford: Oxford University Press, 2005), p. 139.
25. Kovel, *The Enemy of Nature*, p. 2.
26. Vandana Shiva, 'New Emperors, Old Clothes', *The Ecologist*, 1 July 2005.
27. Ibid.
28. Ibid.
29. Michael Reed, *The Landscape of Britain: From the Beginnings to 1914* (London: Routledge, 1997), p. 242.
30. Peter Robinson, 'Take It to the Limits: Milton Friedman on Libertarianism', *Uncommon Knowledge*, 10 February 1999.
31. Kovel, *The Enemy of Nature*, p. 247.
32. Donald Leech, 'Enclosing Land and Memory in Fifteenth Century Coventry', *Medieval History Journal*, vol. 15, no. 1, 2012.
33. Von Mises, *Human Action*, p. 258.
34. Johan Nylander, 'Sweden the World's 10th Largest Arms Exporter', Agence France Presse, 14 March 2011.
35. Amin, *Ending the Crisis of Capitalism or Ending Capitalism?*, p. 9.
36. Ivo Daalder and James Goldgeier, 'Global NATO', *Foreign Affairs*, vol. 8, no. 5, 2006, p. 105.
37. Don Pittis, 'Solving the Crisis of Too Much Corporate Cash', CBC News, 18 November 2010.
38. Ibid.
39. John Holloway, *Change the World Without Taking Power: The Meaning of Revolution Today* (London: Pluto Press, 2005), p. 195.
40. Harvey, *The New Imperialism*, pp. 145-6.
41. Marx, *Capital*, Volume 1, p. 876.
42. Kovel, *The Enemy of Nature*, pp. 54-5.
43. Johan Galtung, 'The US Economic Crisis: 10 Proposals', Peace and Collaborative Development Network, 29 September 2008.
44. Marx, *Capital*, Volume 1, p. 782.
45. Mike Davis, *Planet of Slums* (London: Verso, 2006), p. 15.
46. Ibid., p. 176.
47. Ibid., p. 202.
48. Michael A. Lebowitz, *Beyond Capital: Marx's Political Economy of the Working Class* (New York: Palgrave MacMillan, 2003), pp. 11-12.
49. Slavoj Žižek, *First as Tragedy, Then as Farce* (London: Verso, 2009), p. 103.
50. Some nations (i.e. South Korea, Taiwan, China, etc.) in the global South have moved closer to so-called First World status, but significant portions of their populations still do not enjoy a standard of living comparable to that in the global North. The city-state of Singapore constitutes a unique case.

51. William I. Robinson, 'Globalisation: Nine Theses on Our Epoch', *Race & Class*, vol. 38, no. 2, 1996, pp. 13–14.
52. Amin, *Ending the Crisis of Capitalism or Ending Capitalism?*, p. 160.
53. Antonio Negri, 'Communism: Some Thoughts on the Concept and Practice', in Costas Douzinas and Slavoj Žižek (eds), *The Idea of Communism* (London: Verso, 2010), p. 156.
54. Marx, *Capital*, Volume 1, p. 799.
55. Mészáros, *The Structural Crisis of Capital*, p. 144.

CHAPTER 3

1. Slavoj Žižek, *Violence* (New York: Picador, 2008), pp. 12–14.
2. Timothy A. Wise, 'The Impacts of U.S. Agricultural Policies on Mexican Producers', in Jonathan Fox and Libby Haight (eds), *Subsidizing Inequality: Mexican Corn Policy Since NAFTA* (Washington, DC: Woodrow Wilson International Center for Scholars, 2010), p. 165.
3. Steve Suppan, 'Mexican Corn, NAFTA and Hunger', Fact Sheet 3, Institute for Agriculture and Trade Policy, Minneapolis MN, May 1996.
4. Wise, 'The Impacts of U.S. Agricultural Policies on Mexican Producers', p. 165.
5. Ibid., p. 166.
6. Ibid., p. 167.
7. Suppan, 'Mexican Corn, NAFTA and Hunger'.
8. Roger Bybee and Carolyn Winter, 'Immigration Flood Unleashed by NAFTA's Disastrous Impact on Mexican Economy', *Common Dreams*, 25 April 2006.
9. Collin Harris, 'NAFTA and the Political Economy of Mexican Migration', *ZNet*, 7 June 2010.
10. David T. Rowlands, 'Mexico: Drug Wars Fuelled by Free Trade', *Green Left Weekly*, 31 October 2010.
11. John Ross, 'Chiapas Under Siege by Global Industries', *NACLA*, 23 February 2009.
12. Ibid.
13. David T. Rowlands, 'Zapatistas Struggle for Another Mexico', *Green Left Weekly*, 27 November 2010.
14. Harris, 'NAFTA and the Political Economy of Mexican Migration'.
15. Ibid.
16. Bybee and Winter, 'Immigration Flood Unleashed by NAFTA's Disastrous Impact on Mexican Economy'.
17. Louis Uchitelle, 'Nafta Should Have Stopped Illegal Immigration, Right?', *New York Times*, 18 February 2007.
18. Jonathan Glennie, 'Land Grabs Have Dominated Colombia's History', *Guardian*, 31 January 2011.
19. For a detailed account of how paramilitarism in Colombia has served the interests of capital, see Jasmin Hristov, *Blood and Capital: The Paramilitarization of Colombia* (Toronto: Between the Lines, 2009).
20. 'Dos millones de personas se han desplazado durante el mandato de Uribe', *El Mercurio*, 6 November 2009.
21. Mike Davis, *Planet of Slums* (London: Verso, 2006), p. 176.

22. G. Lorca, 'NAFTA Behind Mexican Drug Wars', *Latin Daily Financial News*, 23 November 2010.

23. Laura Carlsen, 'The Murdered Women of Juarez', *Foreign Policy in Focus*, 19 January 2011.

24. Leslie Salzinger, 'Manufacturing Sexual Objects: "Harassment," Desire and Discipline on a Maquiladora Shopfloor', *Ethnography*, vol. 1, no. 1, 2000, pp. 74-5.

25. Ibid., p. 80.

26. Daniela Pastrana, 'In Juárez, Years of Seeking Justice for Murdered Women', *Inter Press Service*, 11 June 2010.

27. Joel Kovel, *The Enemy of Nature: The End of Capitalism or the End of the World?* (London: Zed Books, 2007), p. 58.

28. Harris, 'NAFTA and the Political Economy of Mexican Migration'.

29. 'Illegal Immigration: Border-Crossing Deaths Have Doubled Since 1995; Border Patrol's Efforts to Prevent Deaths Have Not Been Fully Evaluated', US Government Accountability Office, Washington DC, August 2006, p. 16.

30. Christine Ahn, Melissa Moore and Nick Parker, 'Migrant Farmworkers: America's New Plantation Workers', Food First, 31 March 2004.

31. 'USAID: Latin American and Caribbean Overview', US Agency for International Development, Washington DC, 2003.

32. Raúl Gutiérrez, 'Progress in Fight on Poverty Called into Question', *Inter Press Service*, 3 July 2007.

33. Benedicte Bull, 'National and International Dimensions of Criminal Violence', Norwegian Peacebuilding Centre, Oslo, April 2011.

34. Martha K. Huggins, 'Urban Violence and Police Privatization in Brazil: Blended Invisibility', *Social Justice*, vol. 27, no. 2, 2000.

35. Evan Williams, 'Death to Undesirables: Brazil's Murder Capital', *Independent*, 15 May 2009.

36. Ibid.

37. John Vidal, 'Farmer Commits Suicide at Protests', *Guardian*, 11 September 2003.

38. P. Sainath, 'Of Luxury Cars and Lowly Tractors', *The Hindu*, 27 December 2010.

39. P. Sainath, 'Neo-Liberal Terrorism in India: The Largest Wave of Suicides in History', *Counterpunch,* 12 February 2009.

40. Vandana Shiva, *Earth Democracy: Justice, Sustainability, and Peace* (Cambridge, MA: South End Press, 2005), p. 91.

41. Milton Friedman, *Capitalism and Freedom* (Chicago: University of Chicago Press, 2002), p. 127.

42. Michael Hardt, 'The Common in Communism', in Costas Douzinas and Slavoj Žižek (eds), *The Idea of Communism* (London: Verso, 2010), p. 137.

43. Deane Curtin, *Chinnagounder's Challenge: The Question of Ecological Citizenship* (Bloomington, IN: Indiana University Press, 1999), pp. 65-6.

44. Shiva, *Earth Democracy*, p. 34.

45. Ibid.

46. Ibid., pp. 77-8.

47. Deepa Bhatia, *Nero's Guests: The Age of Inequality,* Mistral Movies, Tel Aviv, 2009.
48. 'Report of the Expert Group to Advise the Ministry of Rural Development on the Methodology for Conducting the Below Poverty Line (BPL) Census for 11th Five Year Plan', Ministry of Rural Development, Government of India, New Delhi, August 2009.
49. Davis, *Planet of Slums*, pp. 170-71.
50. Bhatia, *Nero's Guests.*
51. Sainath, 'Of Luxury Cars and Lowly Tractors'.
52. Shiva, *Earth Democracy*, p. 127.
53. 'Farmer Suicides in India – Is There a Connection with Bt Cotton', Monsanto Corporation, St Louis MO, 5 December 2008.
54. Gitonga Njeru, 'Climate-related Farmer Suicides Surging in Eastern Kenya', Reuters AlertNet, 12 July 2010.
55. Shiva, *Earth Democracy*, p. 124.

CHAPTER 4

1. Gad J. Heuman and James Walvin, 'The Atlantic Slave Trade: Introduction', in Heuman and Walvin, *The Slavery Reader* (London: Routledge, 2003), p. 4.
2. Food and Agricultural Organization of the United Nations, *The State of Food Insecurity in the World 2005* (Rome: FAO, 2005), p. 20.
3. World Health Organization. 'Global Facts and Figures', United Nations, 2009.
4. Robert E. Black, Simon Cousens, Hope L. Johnson, Joy E. Lawn, Igor Rudan, Diego G. Bassani, Prabhat Jha, Harry Campbell, Christa Fischer Walker, Richard Cibulskis, Thomas Eisele, Li Liu and Colin Mathers, 'Global, Regional, and National Causes of Child Mortality in 2008: A Systematic Analysis', *The Lancet,* 12 May 2008, p. 16.
5. Michael Brie, 'Emancipation and the Left: The Issue of Violence', in Colin Leys and Leo Panitch (eds), *The Socialist Register 2009: Violence Today: Actually Existing Barbarism* (Black Point, NS: Fernwood Publishing, 2009), p. 239.
6. Walden Bello, 'Destroying African Agriculture', Foreign Policy in Focus, 3 June 2008.
7. Ibid.
8. Ibid.
9. John Vidal, 'How Food and Water are Driving a 21st-Century African Land Grab', *Guardian*, 7 March 2010.
10. Robert Albritton, 'Eating the Future: Capitalism Out of Joint', in Robert Albritton, Bob Jessop and Richard Westra (eds), *Political Economy and Global Capitalism: The 21st Century, Present and Future* (London: Anthem Press, 2007), p. 52.
11. Samuel Loewenberg, 'Millions in Niger Facing Food Shortages Once Again', *The Lancet*, 6 May 2006.
12. 'Band-Aids and Beyond: Tackling Disasters in Ethiopia 25 Years After the Famine', Oxfam, 22 October 2009.
13. Loewenberg, 'Millions in Niger Facing Food Shortages Once Again'.

14. Patrick Mulvaney, 'The Dumping-Ground: Africa and GM Food Aid', Open Democracy, 28 April 2004.
15. Martin L. Hirsch, 'Side Effects of Corporate Greed: Pharmaceutical Companies Need a Dose of Corporate Social Responsibility', *Minnesota Journal of Law, Science and Technology*, vol. 9, no. 2, 2008, p. 607.
16. Ibid., pp. 610-11.
17. World Health Organization, 'Research and Development: Coordination and Financing', United Nations, 2010, p. 25.
18. Ibid., p. 29.
19. Hirsch, 'Side Effects of Corporate Greed', p. 611.
20. Sarah Aitken, 'Big Pharma Money Spent on Marketing Exceeds Drug Development Costs', *Natural News*, 22 February 2008.
21. Joe Stephens, 'Panel Faults Pfizer in '96 Clinical Trial in Nigeria', *Washington Post,* 7 May 2006.
22. Ibid.
23. Ibid.
24. Ibid.
25. Joe Stephens, 'Pfizer to Pay $75 million to Settle Nigerian Trovan Drug-Testing Suit', *Washington Post*, 31 July 2009.
26. US Department of State, 'Nigeria: Pfizer Reaches Preliminary Agreement for a $75 Million Settlement', *Guardian*, 20 April 2009.
27. Benjamin Mason Meier, 'International Protection of Persons Undergoing Medical Experimentation: Protecting the Right of Informed Consent', *Berkeley Journal of International Law* 20, 2002, pp. 532-3.
28. Ibid., p. 519.
29. Johanna McGeary, Jay Branigan, William Dowell and Alice Park, 'Paying for AIDS Cocktails', *Time*, 12 February 2001.
30. UN News Centre, 'Life Expectancy in Sub-Saharan Africa is Lower Than 30 Years Ago: UN Index', United Nations, 9 November 2006.
31. Nana K. Poku, 'Poverty, Debt and Africa's HIV/AIDS Crisis', *International Affairs*, vol. 78, no. 3, 2002, p. 533.
32. Joia S. Mukherjee, 'Structural Violence, Poverty and the AIDS Epidemic', *Development*, vol. 50, no. 2, 2007, p. 119.
33. Poku, 'Poverty, Debt and Africa's HIV/AIDS Crisis', pp. 538-9.
34. McGeary et al., 'Paying for AIDS Cocktails'.
35. William W. Fisher III and Cyrill P. Rigamonti, 'The South Africa AIDS Controversy: A Case Study in Patent Law and Policy', Harvard Law School, 10 February 2005, p. 3.
36. Ibid., pp. 7-8.
37. Ibid., p. 8.
38. Amy Nunn, *The Politics and History of AIDS Treatment in Brazil* (New York: Springer, 2009), p. 128.
39. Paulo R. Teixeira, Marco Antonio Vitória and Jhoney Barcarolo, 'The Brazilian Experience in Providing Universal Access to Antiretroviral Therapy', Agence Nationale de Recherches sur le Sida (ANRS), Paris, June 2003, p. 82.
40. Ibid., p. 75.
41. Fisher III and Rigamonti, 'The South Africa AIDS Controversy, p. 10.
42. McGeary et al., 'Paying for AIDS Cocktails'.

43. 'Merck & Co., Inc. Statement on Brazilian Government's Decision to Issue Compulsory License for STOCRIN', Merck & Company, Whitehouse Station NJ, 4 May 2007.
44. 'Fortune 500: Our Annual Rankings of America's Largest Corporations', CNN, 3 May 2010.
45. UNAIDS, 'What Countries Need: Investments Needed for 2010 Targets', United Nations, February 2009.
46. 'Fortune 500'.
47. Naomi Powell, 'World Military Spending Tops $1.6-trillion in 2010', *Globe and Mail*, 11 April 2011.
48. Joia S. Mukherjee, 'Structural Violence, Poverty and the AIDS Epidemic', *Development*, vol. 50, no. 2, 2007, p. 116.
49. UN Department of Public Information, 'Africa and the Millennium Development Goals', United Nations, June 2007.
50. United Nations Economic and Social Council, 'Report on Progress in Reaching the Millennium Development Goals in Africa 2011', United Nations, 8 March 2011, p. 10.
51. Ibid., p. 1.
52. UNICEF, 'The State of the World's Children 2005: Childhood Under Threat', United Nations, December 2004.
53. Joel Kovel, *The Enemy of Nature: The End of Capitalism or the End of the World?* (London: Zed Books, 2007), pp. 152-3.

CHAPTER 5

1. Karl Marx, *Grundrisse: Foundations of the Critique of Political Economy* (London: Penguin, 1993), p. 416.
2. Vandana Shiva, *Earth Democracy: Justice, Sustainability, and Peace* (Cambridge, MA: South End Press, 2005), pp. 32-3.
3. John Bellamy Foster, 'A Failed System: The World Crisis of Capitalist Globalization and its Impact on China', *Monthly Review*, vol. 60, no. 10, 2009.
4. Joel Kovel, *The Enemy of Nature: The End of Capitalism or the End of the World?* (London: Zed Books, 2007), p. 53.
5. Ibid., p. 69.
6. Terry Gibbs and Garry Leech, *The Failure of Global Capitalism: From Cape Breton to Colombia and Beyond* (Sydney, NS: Cape Breton University Press, 2009), p. 121.
7. Brook Larmer, 'Shop, China, Shop', *New York Times* magazine, 30 November 2010.
8. 'Chinese Equivalents', *The Economist*, 24 February 2011.
9. Yuanming Alvin Yao, 'China's Oil Strategy and Its Implications for U.S.-China Relations', Issues & Studies, vol. 42, no. 3, 2006.
10. Tim Flannery, *The Weathermakers: How We Are Changing the Climate and What It Means for Life on Earth* (Toronto: HarperCollins, 2005), p. 74.
11. Walden Bello, 'Will Capitalism Survive Climate Change?', *ZNet*, 7 April 2008.
12. Samir Amin, *Ending the Crisis of Capitalism or Ending Capitalism?* (Cape Town: Pambazuka Press, 2011), p. 34.

13. István Mészáros, *The Structural Crisis of Capital* (New York: Monthly Review Press, 2010), p. 91.
14. Intergovernmental Panel on Climate Change, 'IPCC Fourth Assessment Report: Climate Change 2007', United Nations, 2008.
15. Ibid.
16. United Nations Development Programme, 'Climate Change Threatens Unprecedented Human Development Reversals', United Nations, 27 November 2007.
17. Foster, 'A Failed System'.
18. Mark Schapiro, 'Conning the Climate: Inside the Carbon-Trading Shell Game', *Harper's*, February 2010, p. 31.
19. Peter Evans, 'Carbon Trading No Cure-All', CBC News, 29 April 2010.
20. Schapiro, 'Conning the Climate, p. 34.
21. Ibid., p. 39.
22. Simon Butler, 'Can Capitalism Fix the Climate', *Green Left Weekly*, 11 April 2010.
23. Lee-Anne Broadhead, *International Environmental Politics: The Limits of Green Diplomacy* (London: Lynne Rienner, 2002), p. 95.
24. Kovel, *The Enemy of Nature*, pp. 47–8.
25. Ibid., pp. 89–90.
26. Ian Angus, 'If Socialism Fails: The Spectre of 21st Century Barbarism', *Socialist Voice*, 27 July 2008.

CHAPTER 6

1. Antonio Gramsci, *Selections from the Prison Notebooks* (New York: International Publishers, 1971), p. 259.
2. Ibid., p. 5.
3. Ibid., p. 243.
4. Ibid., p. 259.
5. Ibid., p. 258.
6. David Roberts, *Human Insecurity: Global Structures of Violence* (London: Zed Books, 2008), pp. 70–71.
7. George Lambie, *The Cuban Revolution in the 21st Century* (London: Pluto Press, 2010), p. 112.
8. Alan Maass, *The Case for Socialism* (Chicago: Haymarket Books, 2010), p. 123.
9. Michel Foucault, 'The Means of Correct Training', in Paul Rabinow (ed.), *The Foucault Reader* (New York: Vintage Books, 1984), p. 197.
10. Robert McChesney, *The Political Economy of Media: Enduring Issues, Emerging Dilemmas* (New York: Monthly Review Press, 2008), p. 27.
11. Ibid., pp. 131–2.
12. Ibid., p. 112.
13. 'Americans on Iraq and the UN Inspections II', PIPA/Knowledge Networks Poll, 21 February 2003.
14. Secretary-General Kofi Annan, 'Excerpts: Annan Interview', BBC News, 16 September 2004.
15. Maass, *The Case for Socialism*, p. 123.
16. Paul Farmer, 'An Anthropology of Structural Violence, *Current Anthropology*, vol. 45, no. 3, 2004, p. 308.

17. Sue L.T. McGregor, 'Consumerism as a Source of Structural Violence', Human Sciences Working Paper Archive, East Lansing MI, 2003.
18. Samir Amin, *Ending the Crisis of Capitalism or Ending Capitalism?* (Cape Town: Pambazuka Press, 2011), p. 15.
19. Slavoj Žižek, *Violence* (New York: Picador, 2008), pp. 21-2.
20. Ibid., p. 22.
21. Eric Toussaint, 'Transfers from the Periphery to the Centre, from Labour to Capital', Committee for the Abolition of the Third World Debt, 7 January 2004, pp. 5-6.
22. Edward J. Mills, Steve Kanters, Nick Bansback, Jean Nachega, Mark Alberton, Christopher G. Au-Yeung, Andy Mtambo, Ivy L. Bourgeault, Samuel Luboga, Robert S. Hogg, and Nathan Ford, 'The Financial Cost of Doctors Emigrating from Sub-Saharan Africa: Human Capital Analysis', *British Medical Journal*, 24 November 2011.
23. Geoffrey York, 'Brain Drain of African Doctors Saved Canada $400 Million', *Globe and Mail*, 26 November 2011.
24. Ernesto 'Che' Guevara, 'Socialism and the Man in Cuba', in David Deutschmann (ed.), *Che Guevara Reader: Writings on Politics and Revolution* (Melbourne: Ocean Press, 2003), p. 215.
25. Marx's definition of 'petty bourgeois' was not precise; it appeared to identify an attitude as much as a class status.
26. Amin, *Ending the Crisis of Capitalism or Ending Capitalism?*, p. 177.
27. Joel Kovel, *The Enemy of Nature: The End of Capitalism or the End of the World?* (London: Zed Books, 2007), p. 121.
28. 'US Extends Drone Strikes to Somalia', Al Jazeera, 1 July 2011.
29. Amin, *Ending the Crisis of Capitalism or Ending Capitalism?*, p. 2.

CHAPTER 7

1. István Mészáros, *The Structural Crisis of Capital* (New York: Monthly Review Press, 2010), p. 37.
2. Colin Cremin, *Capitalism's New Clothes: Enterprise, Ethics and Enjoyment in Times of Crisis* (London: Pluto Press, 2011), p. 79.
3. Mészáros, *The Structural Crisis of Capital*, pp. 89-90.
4. Slavoj Žižek, *First as Tragedy, Then as Farce* (London: Verso, 2009), p. 140.
5. Mészáros, *The Structural Crisis of Capital*, p. 176.
6. John Holloway, *Change the World Without Taking Power: The Meaning of Revolution Today* (London: Pluto Press, 2005), p. 229.
7. 'Set Up a Social Enterprise', Department for Business Innovation and Skills, London, July 2011.
8. Alan Maass, *The Case for Socialism* (Chicago: Haymarket Books, 2010), p. 73.
9. Michael A. Lebowitz, *The Socialist Alternative: Real Human Development* (New York: Monthly Review Press, 2010), p. 111.
10. Ibid., p. 131.
11. Samir Amin, *Ending the Crisis of Capitalism or Ending Capitalism?* (Cape Town: Pambazuka Press, 2011), p. 18.
12. Joel Kovel, *The Enemy of Nature: The End of Capitalism or the End of the World?* (London: Zed Books, 2007), p. 163.

13. Lebowitz, *The Socialist Alternative*, p. 86.
14. Kovel, *The Enemy of Nature*, p. 218.
15. Mészáros, *The Structural Crisis of Capital*, p. 143.
16. George Lambie, *The Cuban Revolution in the 21st Century* (London: Pluto Press, 2010), pp. 97-8.
17. Marta Harnecker, *Rebuilding the Left* (London: Zed Books, 2007), p. 88.
18. Lebowitz, *The Socialist Alternative*, p. 60.
19. Ellen Meiksins Wood, *The Retreat from Class: A New 'True' Socialism* (London: Verso, 1998), p. 135.
20. Michael A. Lebowitz, *Beyond Capital: Marx's Political Economy of the Working Class* (New York: Palgrave MacMillan, 2003), p. 131.
21. Lebowitz, *The Socialist Alternative*, pp. 119-20.
22. Kevin B. Anderson, *Marx at the Margins: On Nationalism, Ethnicity, and Non-Western Societies* (Chicago: University of Chicago Press, 2010), pp. 144-5.
23. Ibid., p. 3.
24. Ibid., p. 3.
25. Ibid., p. 224.
26. Ibid., p. 226.
27. Mészáros, *The Structural Crisis of Capital*, p. 92.
28. Amin, *Ending the Crisis of Capitalism or Ending Capitalism?*, p. 2.
29. Mészáros, *The Structural Crisis of Capital*, pp. 131-2.
30. George Lambie, *The Cuban Revolution in the 21st Century* (London: Pluto Press, 2010), p. 244.
31. Hugo Chávez, 'Do We Want to End Poverty? Let Us Empower the Poor (The Venezuelan Experience)', United Nations, 20 September 2004.
32. Lisandro Pérez, interview with author, Caracas, Venezuela, 29 April 2005.
33. Maass, *The Case for Socialism*, p. 79.
34. Kovel, *The Enemy of Nature*, p. 272.
35. Terry Gibbs, 'Business as Unusual: What the Chávez Era Tells Us About Democracy Under Globalisation', *Third World Quarterly*, vol. 27, no. 2, 2006, p. 268.
36. Naomi Klein, *The Shock Doctrine: The Rise of Disaster Capitalism* (London: Metropolitan Books, 2007), pp. 453-4.
37. Tom Malleson, 'Cooperatives and the "Bolivarian Revolution" in Venezuela', *Affinities: A Journal of Radical Theory, Culture, and Action*, vol. 4, no. 1, 2010, p. 158.
38. Ibid., p. 156.
39. Ibid., p. 160.
40. 'Social Program Has Benefitted Nearly 100,000 Women', Ministry of People's Power for Foreign Affairs, 28 June 2011.
41. Mark Weisbrot, 'Poverty Reduction in Venezuela: A Reality-Based View', *ReVista: Harvard Review of Latin America*, Fall 2008. See also Tamara Pearson, 'Poverty and Inequality Decline in Venezuela, *Venezuela Analysis*, 24 December 2008.
42. Pearson, 'Poverty and Inequality Decline in Venezuela'.
43. Arnaldo Sotillo, interview with author, Caracas, Venezuela, 17 May 2005.

44. National Institute of Statistics, Bolivarian Republic of Venezuela, 19 September 2005.

45. Humberto Márquez, 'Venezuela Declares Itself Illiteracy-Free', Inter Press Service, 28 October 2005.

46. Lisandro Pérez, interview with author.

47. See Corporación Latinobarómetro, *Informe 2010* (Santiago, Chile: Corporación Latinobarómetro, 2010).

48. Ibid., p. 26.

49. Ibid., p. 41.

50. Lambie, *The Cuban Revolution in the 21st Century*, p. 242.

51. Kaia Lai, 'Petrocaribe: Chávez's Venturesome Solution to the Caribbean Oil Crisis', Council on Hemispheric Affairs, Washington DC, 31 December 2006.

52. 'The Resignation of Rafael Correa, Ecuador's Economy Minister: An Example of IFI's Influence', IFIs Latin American Monitor, 22 August 2005.

53. Annabella Quiroga, 'Acuerdo del Banco del Sur sobre el capital', *Clarín*, 28 June 2008.

54. Žižek, *First as Tragedy, Then as Farce*, p. 102.

55. Lambie, *The Cuban Revolution in the 21st Century*, pp. 144-5.

56. Emilio Duharte Díaz, 'Cuba at the Onset of the 21st Century: Socialism, Democracy, and Political Reforms', *Socialism and Democracy*, vol. 24, no. 3, 2010.

57. Lambie, *The Cuban Revolution in the 21st Century*, pp. 162-7.

58. Robert Buddan, 'Cuba's Embargoed Democracy', *Jamaica Gleaner*, 11 November 2007.

59. Similarly, in most parliamentary systems (e.g. Britain and Canada) the prime minister is not elected directly by the people. A prime minister is chosen by their political party and must be an elected Member of Parliament.

60. Buddan, 'Cuba's Embargoed Democracy'.

61. Lambie, *The Cuban Revolution in the 21st Century*, p. 180.

62. Ibid., p. 164.

63. Ibid., p. 165.

64. Ibid., p. 67.

65. Patricia Grogg, 'Cuba's Communist Party to Adopt Reforms', Inter Press Service, 15 April 2011.

66. Lambie, *The Cuban Revolution in the 21st Century*, pp. 167-8.

67. In actuality, barely 50 per cent of the voting-age population casts ballots for candidates of the Republican and Democratic parties in presidential election years, and only some 35 per cent in mid-term elections. See 'Voting and Registration' on the website of the US Census Bureau.

68. Lambie, *The Cuban Revolution in the 21st Century*, p. 175.

69. Ibid., p. 190.

70. Ibid., pp. 188-9.

71. Ibid., p. 190.

72. Buddan, 'Cuba's Embargoed Democracy'.

73. Lambie, *The Cuban Revolution in the 21st Century*, p. 217.

74. Michael Voss, 'Cuba Pushes its "Medical Diplomacy"', BBC News, 20 May 2009.
75. Andres Schipani, 'Revolutionary Care: Castro's Doctors Give Hope to the Children of Chernobyl', *Guardian,* 2 July 2009.
76. Lambie, *The Cuban Revolution in the 21st Century,* p. 218.
77. Frida Berrigan, 'Weapons: Our #1 Export?' *Foreign Policy in Focus,* 30 June 2009. The majority of US weapons sales over the past decade went to countries that the US State Department defined as undemocratic and/or major human rights abusers.
78. Lambie, *The Cuban Revolution in the 21st Century,* pp. 202-3.
79. Steve Sternberg, '18,000 Deaths Blamed on Lack of Insurance', *USA Today,* 22 May 2002.
80. 'Cuba: U.S. Aid Worker Alan Gross's Trial Ends', BBC News, 5 March 2011.
81. *Amnesty International Report 2010: The State of the World's Human Rights,* Amnesty International, London, 2010. See also Michael Voss, 'Number of Cuban Political Prisoners Dips', BBC News online, 5 July 2010.
82. Federico Fuentes, 'Colombia: Doing Business, Killing Workers', *Green Left Weekly,* 13 November 2010. State security forces in Colombia have also perpetrated more than 2,000 extrajudicial executions since 2002, while more than 38,000 people have 'disappeared' in the past four years and there are 4.5 million internally displaced persons in the country.
83. Lambie, *The Cuban Revolution in the 21st Century,* p. 195.
84. John Bellamy Foster, 'A Failed System: The World Crisis of Capitalist Globalization and its Impact on China', *Monthly Review,* vol. 60, no. 10, 2009.
85. Kovel, *The Enemy of Nature,* pp. 226-9.
86. Ibid., p. 243.
87. Ian Angus, 'Ecosocialism and the Fight Against Global Warming', *Socialist Voice,* 3 December 2007.
88. 'Bolivia Celebrates Law Granting Rights to Mother Earth', Environmental News Service, 20 April 2011.
89. Mattia Cabitza, 'Will Bolivia Make the Breakthrough on Food Security and the Environment?' *Guardian,* 20 June 2011.
90. Neville Spencer, 'Cuban Permaculturalist: How Cuba Made a "Green Revolution",' *Green Left Weekly,* 25 April 2008.
91. Ibid.
92. Steve Whysall, 'The City of the Future Will Be a Farm, According to Ecologist David Tracey', *Vancouver Sun,* 28 April 2011.
93. Lambie, *The Cuban Revolution in the 21st Century,* p. 183.
94. Faith Morgan, *The Power of Community: How Cuba Survived Peak Oil* (Yellow Springs, OH: Community Service, 2006).
95. *Living Planet Report 2006,* World Wildlife Fund, Godalming, 2006, p. 19.
96. Ibid.
97. Neville Spencer, 'Cuban Permaculturalist: How Cuba Made a "Green Revolution",' *Green Left Weekly,* 25 April 2008.
98. Kovel, *The Enemy of Nature,* p. 241.

99. Hugo Prieto, Interview with Edgardo Lander: The Path for Venezuela Can Not Be Neoliberalism or Stalinism', Venezuela Analysis, 7 April 2011.
100. Karl Marx, *Capital: A Critique of Political Economy*, Volume 3 (Moscow: Progress Publishers, 1959), p. 776.

CONCLUSION

1. Samir Amin, *Ending the Crisis of Capitalism or Ending Capitalism?* (Cape Town: Pambazuka Press, 2011), pp. 105-6.
2. Ibid., p. 38.
3. István Mészáros, *The Structural Crisis of Capital* (New York: Monthly Review Press, 2010), p. 170.
4. Amin, *Ending the Crisis of Capitalism or Ending Capitalism?*, p. 124.
5. Joel Kovel, *The Enemy of Nature: The End of Capitalism or the End of the World?* (London: Zed Books, 2007), p. 205.
6. Karl Marx and Friedrich Engels, *The German Ideology* (New York: Prometheus Books, 1998), p. 60.
7. Kovel, *The Enemy of Nature*, pp. 219-20.
8. Amin, *Ending the Crisis of Capitalism or Ending Capitalism?*, p. 183.
9. Robert McChesney, *The Political Economy of Media: Enduring Issues, Emerging Dilemmas* (New York: Monthly Review Press, 2008), p. 17.
10. Amin, *Ending the Crisis of Capitalism or Ending Capitalism?*, p. 184.
11. Ernesto 'Che' Guevara, 'Socialism and the Man in Cuba', in David Deutschmann (ed.), *Che Guevara Reader: Writings on Politics and Revolution* (Melbourne: Ocean Press, 2003), p. 216.
12. Ibid., p. 220.
13. Ibid., p. 221.
14. Paulo Freire, *Pedagogy of the Oppressed* (New York: Continuum, 2000), p. 55.
15. George Lambie, *The Cuban Revolution in the 21st Century* (London: Pluto Press, 2010), p. 228.
16. Mészáros, *The Structural Crisis of Capital*, p. 133.
17. Slavoj Žižek, *First as Tragedy, Then as Farce* (London: Verso, 2009), p. 156.

BIBLIOGRAPHY

Ahmed, N.M. (2007) 'Structural Violence as a Form of Genocide: The Impact of the International Economic Order'. *Entelequia: Revista Interdisciplinar* 5, pp. 3–41.

Ahn, C., M. Moore and N. Parker (2004) 'Migrant Farmworkers: America's New Plantation Workers'. Food First, 31 March.

Albritton, R. (2007) 'Eating the Future: Capitalism Out of Joint. In R. Albritton, R. Jessop and R. Westra (eds), *Political Economy and Global Capitalism: The 21st Century, Present and Future*. London: Anthem Press.

Amin, S. (2011) *Ending the Crisis of Capitalism or Ending Capitalism?* Cape Town: Pambazuka Press.

Amnesty International. (2010) *Amnesty International Report 2010: The State of the World's Human Rights*. London: Amnesty International.

Anderson, K.B. (2010) *Marx at the Margins: On Nationalism, Ethnicity, and Non-Western Societies*. Chicago: University of Chicago Press.

Angus, I. (2008) 'If Socialism Fails: The Spectre of 21st Century Barbarism'. *Socialist Voice*, 27 July.

Bello, W. (2008) 'Destroying African Agriculture'. Foreign Policy in Focus, 3 June.

Bhatia, D. (2009) *Nero's Guests: The Age of Inequality* [documentary film]. India: Mistral Movies.

Black, R.E., S. Cousens, H.L. Johnson, J.E. Lawn, I. Rudan, D.G. Bassani, P. Jha, H. Campbell, C. F. Walker, R. Cibulskis, T. Eisele, L. Liu and Colin Mathers (2008) 'Global, Regional, and National Causes of Child Mortality in 2008: A Systematic Analysis'. *The Lancet*, 12 May.

Boron, A. (1995) *State, Capitalism, and Democracy in Latin America*. Boulder, CO: Lynne Reinner.

Brie. M. (2009) 'Emancipation and the Left: The Issue of Violence'. In C. Leys and L. Panitch (eds), *The Socialist Register 2009: Violence Today: Actually Existing Barbarism*, Black Point, NS: Fernwood Publishing.

174 CAPITALISM

Broadhead, L. (2002) *International Environmental Politics: The Limits of Green Diplomacy*. London: Lynne Rienner.

Carlsen, L. (2011) 'The Murdered Women of Juarez'. Foreign Policy in Focus, 19 January.

Chávez, H. (2004), 'Do We Want to End Poverty? Let Us Empower the Poor (The Venezuelan Experience)'. Meeting of Heads of State, United Nations, 20 September.

Chomsky, N. (1998) *Profit Over People: Neoliberalism and Global Order*. New York: Seven Stories Press.

Corporación Latinobarómetro (2010) *Informe 2010*. Santiago: Corporación Latinobarómetro.

Cremin, C. (2011) *Capitalism's New Clothes: Enterprise, Ethics and Enjoyment in Times of Crisis*. London: Pluto Press.

Curtin, D. (1999) *Chinnagounder's Challenge: The Question of Ecological Citizenship*. Bloomington: Indiana University Press.

Daalder, I., and J. Goldgeier (2006) 'Global NATO'. *Foreign Affairs*, vol. 85, no. 5.

Davis, M. (2006) *Planet of Slums*. London: Verso.

Duharte Díaz, E. (2010) 'Cuba at the Onset of the 21st Century: Socialism, Democracy, and Political Reforms'. *Socialism and Democracy*, vol. 24, no. 3.

Ellner, S. (2008) *Rethinking Venezuelan Politics: Class, Conflict, and the Chávez Phenomenon*. Boulder, CO: Lynne Rienner.

Farmer, P. (2001) *Infections and Inequalities: The Modern Plagues*. Berkeley: University of California Press.

Farmer, P. (2004) 'An Anthropology of Structural Violence'. *Current Anthropology*, vol. 45, no. 3.

Fisher III, W.W., and C.P. Rigamonti (2005) 'The South Africa AIDS Controversy: A Case Study in Patent Law and Policy'. Harvard Law School, 10 February.

Foster, J.B. (2009) 'A Failed System: The World Crisis of Capitalist Globalization and its Impact on China'. *Monthly Review*, vol. 60, no. 10.

Freire, P. (2000) *Pedagogy of the Oppressed*. New York: Continuum.

Friedman, M. (2002) *Capitalism and Freedom*. Chicago: University of Chicago Press.

Galtung, J. (1969) 'Violence, Peace, and Peace Research'. *Journal of Peace Research*, vol. 6, no. 3.

Galtung, J. (1990) 'Cultural Violence'. *Journal of Peace Research*, vol. 27, no. 3.

Galtung, J. (2002) 'A World in Economic Crisis'. DIR & Institute for History, International and Social Studies, Aalborg University.

Galtung, J. (2008) 'The U.S. Economic Crisis: 10 Proposals'. Peace and Collaborative Development Network, 29 September.

Gibbs, T. (2006) 'Business as Unusual: What the Chávez Era Tells Us About Democracy Under Globalisation'. *Third World Quarterly*, vol. 27, no. 2.

Gibbs, T., and G. Leech (2009) *The Failure of Global Capitalism: From Cape Breton to Colombia and Beyond*. Sydney, NS: Cape Breton University Press.

Gramsci, A. (1971) *Selections from the Prison Notebooks*. New York: International Publishers.

Guevara, E. (2003) 'Socialism and the Man in Cuba', in D. Deutschmann (ed.), *Che Guevara Reader: Writings on Politics and Revolution*. Melbourne: Ocean Press.

Hardt, M. (2010) 'The Common in Communism'. in C. Douzinas and S. Žižek (eds), *The Idea of Communism*, London: Verso.

Harnecker, M. (2007) *Rebuilding the Left*. London: Zed Books.

Harvey, D. (2005) *The New Imperialism*. Oxford: Oxford University Press.

Hayek, F.A. (1962) 'The Moral Element in Free Enterprise'. *The Freeman: Ideas on Liberty*, vol. 12, no. 7.

Hirsch, M.L. (2008) 'Side Effects of Corporate Greed: Pharmaceutical Companies Need a Dose of Corporate Social Responsibility'. *Minnesota Journal of Law, Science and Technology*, vol. 9, no. 2.

Ho, K. (2007) 'Structural Violence as a Human Rights Violation'. *Essex Human Rights Review*, vol. 4, no. 2.

Holloway, J. (2005) *Change the World Without Taking Power: The Meaning of Revolution Today*. London: Pluto Press.

Hristov, J. (2009) *Blood and Capital: The Paramilitarization of Colombia*. Toronto: Between the Lines.

Indian Ministry of Rural Development (2009) 'Report of the Expert Group to Advise the Ministry of Rural Development on the Methodology for Conducting the Below Poverty Line (BPL) Census for 11th Five Year Plan'. New Delhi, August.

Jacques, K. (2000) 'Environmental Justice Case Study: Texaco's Oil Production in the Ecuadorian Rainforest'. University of Michigan.

Kapitza, S.P. (2009) 'Global Population Blow-Up and After: The Demographic Revolution and Sustainable Development'. *Bulletin of the Georgian National Academy of Sciences*, vol. 3, no.1.

Kiernan, B. (2005) 'Letting Sudan Get Away with Murder'. *Yale Global Online*. 4 February.

Klein, N. (2007) *The Shock Doctrine: The Rise of Disaster Capitalism*. London: Metropolitan Books.

Kovel, J. (2007) *The Enemy of Nature: The End of Capitalism or the End of the World?* London: Zed Books.

Lai, K. (2006) 'Petrocaribe: Chávez's Venturesome Solution to the Caribbean Oil Crisis'. Council on Hemispheric Affairs, Washington DC, 31 December.

Lambie, G. (2010) *The Cuban Revolution in the 21st Century*. London: Pluto Press.

Lebowitz, M.A. (2003) *Beyond Capital: Marx's Political Economy of the Working Class*. New York: Palgrave Macmillan.

Lebowitz, M.A. (2010) *The Socialist Alternative: Real Human Development*. New York: Monthly Review Press.

Leech, D. (2012) 'Enclosing Land and Memory in Fifteenth Century Coventry'. *Medieval History Journal*, vol. 15, no. 1.

Malleson, T. (2010) 'Cooperatives and the "Bolivarian Revolution" in Venezuela'. *Affinities: A Journal of Radical Theory, Culture, and Action*, vol. 4, no. 1.

Marx, K. (1959) *Capital: A Critique of Political Economy*, Volume 3. Moscow: Progress Publishers.

Marx, K. (1992) *Capital: A Critique of Political Economy*, Volume 1. London: Penguin.

Marx, K. (1993) *Grundrisse*. New York: Penguin.

Marx, K., and F. Engels (1992) *The Communist Manifesto*. New York: Bantam Books.

Marx, K., and F. Engels (1998) *The German Ideology*. New York: Prometheus Books.

McChesney, R. (2008) *The Political Economy of Media: Enduring Issues, Emerging Dilemmas*. New York: Monthly Review Press.

McCormack, G. (2003) 'Reflections on Modern Japanese History in the Context of the Concept of Genocide', in R. Gellately and B. Kiernan (eds), *The Specter of Genocide: Mass Murder in Historical Perspective*. Cambridge: Cambridge University Press.

McGregor, S.L.T. (2003) 'Consumerism as a Source of Structural Violence'. Human Sciences Working Paper Archive, East Lansing, MI.

Meier, B.M. (2002) 'International Protection of Persons Undergoing Medical Experimentation: Protecting the Right of Informed Consent'. *Berkeley Journal of International Law* 20.

Mészáros. I. (2010) *The Structural Crisis of Capital*. New York: Monthly Review Press.

Mises, L. von. (1996) *Human Action: A Treatise on Economics*. San Francisco: Fox & Wilkes.

Mises, L. von. (2006) 'The Causes of the Economic Crisis: An address' in P.L. Greaves, Jr. (ed.), *The Causes of the Economic Crisis, and Other Essays Before and After the Great Depression*. Auburn, AL: Ludwig von Mises Institute.

Morgan, F. (2006) *The Power of Community: How Cuba Survived Peak Oil* [documentary film]. Yellow Springs OH: Community Service.Mukherjee, J.S. (2007) 'Structural Violence, Poverty and the AIDS Epidemic'. *Development*, vol. 50, no. 2.

Negri, A. (2010) 'Communism: Some Thoughts on the Concept and Practice', in C. Douzinas and S. Žižek (eds), *The Idea of Communism*. London: Verso.

Nunn, A. (2009) *The Politics and History of AIDS Treatment in Brazil*. New York: Springer.

Poku, N.K. (2002) 'Poverty, Debt and Africa's HIV/AIDS Crisis'. *International Affairs*, vol. 78, no. 3.

Prieto, H. (2011) Interview with Edgardo Lander: The Path for Venezuela Can Not Be Neoliberalism or Stalinism', *Venezuela Analysis*, 7 April.

Reed, M. (1997) *The Landscape of Britain: From the Beginnings to 1914*. London: Routledge.

Roberts. D. (2008) *Human Insecurity: Global Structures of Violence*. London: Zed Books.

Robinson, P. (1999) 'Take it to the Limits: Milton Friedman on Libertarianism'. *Uncommon Knowledge*, 10 February.

Robinson, W.I. (1996) 'Globalisation: Nine Theses on our Epoch'. *Race & Class*, vol. 38, no. 2.

Salzinger, L. (2000) 'Manufacturing Sexual Objects: "Harassment", Desire and Discipline on a Maquiladora Shopfloor'. *Ethnography*, vol. 1, no. 1.

Sawyer, S. (2004) *Crude Chronicles: Indigenous Politics, Multinational Oil, and Neoliberalism in Ecuador*. Durham, NC: Duke University Press.

Schaack, B. V. (1997) 'The Crime of Political Genocide: Repairing the Genocide Convention's Blind Spot'. *Yale Law Journal*, vol. 106, no. 7.

Schabas, W.A. (2008) 'Genocide Law in a Time of Transition: Recent Developments in the Law of Genocide'. *Rutgers Law Review*, vol. 61, no. 1.

Selfa, L. (1997) 'Mexico After the Zapatista Uprising'. *International Socialism* 75.

Shiva, V. (2005) *Earth Democracy: Justice, Sustainability, and Peace*. Cambridge, MA: South End Press.

Stanford, J. (2008) *Economics for Everyone: A Short Guide to the Economics of Capitalism*. Halifax, NS: Fernwood Publishing.

Staub, E. (2002) 'The Roots of Evil: The Origins of Genocide and Other Group Violence'. Cambridge: Cambridge University Press.

Suppan, S. (1996) 'Mexican Corn, NAFTA and Hunger'. Fact Sheet 3. Institute for Agriculture and Trade Policy, Minneapolis, May.

Teixeira, P., M.A. Vitória and J. Barcarolo (2003) 'The Brazilian Experience in Providing Universal Access to Antiretroviral Therapy'. Agence Nationale de Recherches sur le Sida, June.

Toussaint, E. (2004) 'Transfers from the Periphery to the Centre, from Labour to Capital'. Unpublished Paper, Committee for the Abolition of the Third World Debt.

Travis, H. (2010) *Genocide in the Middle East: The Ottoman Empire, Iraq, and Sudan*. Durham, NC: Carolina Academic Press.

United Nations (1947) 'First Draft of the Genocide Convention'. UN Secretariat, May.

United Nations (1951) 'Convention on the Prevention and Punishment of the Crime of Genocide'. Office of the High Commissioner for Human Rights, 12 January.

United Nations (1999) 'Rome Statute of the International Criminal Court'. United Nations Treaty Collection, 12 July.

United Nations (2004) 'The State of the World's Children 2005: Childhood Under Threat'. United Nations Children's Fund (UNICEF), December.

United Nations (2005) *The State of Food Insecurity in the World 2005*, Food and Agricultural Organization of the United Nations.

United Nations (2007) 'Africa and the Millennium Development Goals'. United Nations Department of Public Information, June.

United Nations (2007) 'Climate Change Threatens Unprecedented Human Development Reversals'. United Nations Development Programme (UNDP), 27 November.

United Nations (2008) 'Global Health Observatory Data Repository'. World Health Organization.

United Nations (2009) *Global Facts and Figures*. World Health Organization.

United Nations (2009) 'What Countries Need: Investments Needed for 2010 Targets'. UNAIDS, February.

United Nations (2010) 'Research and Development: Coordination and Financing'. World Health Organization.

United Nations (2011) 'Report on Progress in Reaching the Millennium Development Goals in Africa, 2011'. United Nations Economic and Social Council, 8 March.

US Government (2006) 'Illegal Immigration: Border-Crossing Deaths Have Doubled Since 1995; Border Patrol's Efforts to Prevent Deaths Have Not Been Fully Evaluated'. US Government Accountability Office, Washington DC, August.

Weisbrot, M. (2008) 'Poverty Reduction in Venezuela: A Reality-Based View'. *ReVista: Harvard Review of Latin America*, Fall.

Wise, T.A. (2010) 'The Impacts of U.S. Agricultural Policies on Mexican Producers', in J. Fox and L. Haight (eds), *Subsidizing Inequality: Mexican Corn Policy since NAFTA*. Washington, DC: Woodrow Wilson International Center for Scholars.

Wood, E.M. (1998) *The Retreat from Class: A New 'True' Socialism*. London: Verso.

World Wildlife Fund (2006) *Living Planet Report 2006*. Godalming: WWF.

Žižek, S. (2008) *Violence*. New York: Picador.

Žižek, S. (2009) *First as Tragedy, Then as Farce*. London: Verso.

INDEX

Assembly voting procedures, 133;
organic agriculture, 145;
participatory democracy, 134;
'Special Period', 137; urban
agriculture, 146; US economic
embargo, 34, 136, 138; US
vilification of, 140; Venezuela
'barter', 129
Curtin, Deane, 58

Davis, Mike, 39, 49
death squads, Latin American, 54
debt, 61; farmer, 59-60; global
South, 103-4; Indian peasant, 56;
servicing, 66
democracy: global democratic
deficit, 83; internalized capitalist,
113
Democratic Republic of the Congo,
China land lease, 67
dependency theory, 28
Dervis, Kermal, 89
'development', 10
dollar-gold standard delinking, 35
drugs, *see* antiretroviral drugs
Duharte Díaz, Emilio, 132

ecological sustainability, 86, 143,
145
ecosocialism, 144; approaches, 8
Ecuador, 87, 129; Venezuelan loan,
129
education, consent role, 97;
institutional structure, 98;
Venezuelan transformation, 126
El Salvador, 42, 142; continued
emigration, 53
elite(s): capitalist, 25, 95, 104, 124;
China and India, 87; global South
domestic, 34, 106; ruling, 94, 99;
ruling, discourse, 96
Enclosure Acts, Britain, 150
enclosure process, 30; British Acts,
150; intellectual property rights,
37
Engels, Friedrich, 28
Ethiopia, farmland leased, 66
export model; crops, 65-6;
neoliberal, 58
Exxon Valdez disaster, 3

Farmer, Paul, 10, 101
farmer suicides, 6, 44, 60-61, 62;
India, 55, 56; Kenya, 89
FDA (US Food and Drug Agency),
overseas testing regulations, 72
female genital mutilation, 8
femicide, Juárez, 50-51
financial markets: deregulated, 35;
2008 bubble burst, 36
food aid, US shipping companies
lobby, 67-8
Food First, 52
food self-sufficiency, 144
Fordist compact, dismantled, 32, 83
foreign aid, 103
Foster, John Bellamy, 86
Foucault, Michel, 98
France, publicly funded drug
research bias, 70
France, Anatole, 27
free-market capitalism, dictatorship
compatible, 24
Freire, Paulo, 11, 155
Friedman, Milton, 23-4, 26, 30-31,
57; democracy concept, 25

Galtung, Johan, 4, 9-11, 20, 38, 42
Gandhi, Mohandas, 42
Gates, Bill, 102
GATT (General Agreement on
Tariffs and Trade), Uruguay
Round, 57
GDP (gross domestic product), 30
gender equality, Cuban parliament,
133
Geneva Convention, Article 2(c),
15
genocide: ICC definition, 15;
indigenous Americans, 12;
selective highlighting, 42
Germany, publicly funded drug
research bias, 70
Gibbs, Terry, 124
global depression, post-2008, 35
global energy use, USA, 87
global North-South wealth gap, 29
global South: cheaper inputs,
capitalist need, 29; climate
change impact, 90; communal
social organization, 119;

dismantled, 32-3, 83, 95, 109-10
Khymer Rouge genocide, 17-18
Kiernan, Ben, 16, 18
Klein, Naomi, 124
Kovel, Joel, 19, 22, 31, 37, 51, 83, 86,
  92-3, 105, 114-15, 123, 136, 143-4,
  146, 151
Kyoto Protocol, 90

Lage, Carlos, 137
Lambie, George, 96, 116, 121, 133-5,
  140, 146, 156
Lander, Edgardo, 147
Lantos, Tom, 72
Latin America, 49; agrarian
  societies, 119; class-based
  apartheid system, 54; land
  dispossession, 55; multinational
  mining corporations, 48;
  radicalization, 120;
  transformation, 156; water
  availability, 89
'Law of Mother Earth', Bolivia, 144
Lebowitz, Michael, 113, 115-17;
  'Charter for Human Development',
  112
Lee Kyung Hae, self-stabbing, 55
Leech, Donald, 31
liberal democracy, 23-4, 31, 110;
  role of, 26
'liberal' government, international
  level, 34
Libya, 106
life expectancy, Cuba, 137
'lifestyle' drugs, 69-70
Liggeri, Enrico, 72
literacy, Venezuela projects, 127,
  138
Luxemburg, Rosa, 157

Maass, Alan, 97, 100, 112, 123
malaria, 70
Malleson, Tom, 125
Mandel, Ernest, 149
Mann, Michael, 19
maquiladoras: El Salvador, 53; job
  creation and losses, 47; sexist
  hiring practices, 50; sexual
  harassment, 51
market economy, 22

Marx, Karl, 21-2, 28, 37-9, 41, 85,
  117, 119-20, 147-8, 152; later
  works, 118; 'primitive
  accumulation', 29
McCarthy witch hunt, USA, 155
McChesney, Robert, 25, 98-9, 153
McDonald, Patrick, 64
McGregor, Sue, 101
Mészáros, István, 41, 88, 102,
  108-9, 115, 119-20, 129, 151, 156
means of production, social
  ownership, 113-16, 134, 148
media, corporate concentration,
  97-8
Meier, Benjamin Mason, 73
Meiksins Wood, Ellen, 117
Merck: AIDS drugs, 'discounts', 78;
  R&D costs narrative, 79
Merida Initiative (Plan Mexico), 50
Mexico: Constitution Article 27
  repealed, 44, 46; drug cartels-
  Army violence, 6, 49; farmer
  dispossession, 5, 43; farmers
  quitting, 46; infant and child
  mortality rate, 137; land
  dispossession, 55; manufacturing
  employment fall, 48
middle class, China growth, 87-8
migrant farm workers, USA, 52
military-industrial complex, USA,
  107
Millennium Development Goals,
  80-81
Miller, Judith, 99-100
Mission Barrio Adentro, 127
'mixed economy', 32
'modern' world, promises of wealth,
  3
monopolistic practices, capitalist
  reality, 22, 24
Monsanto, 58; farmer suicide
  narrative, 61
Morales, Evo, 143-4
Mossadegh, Mohammad, 106
Mossadeq Ahmed, Nafeez, 18-19
Mukherjee, Joia S., 74, 80
murder rates, northern Mexico, 49

Nader, Ralph, 76
NAFTA (North American Free

Trade Agreement), 5, 43;
Mexican impact, 52; Mexican
drug cartel strengthened, 49;
Mexico industry jobs loss, 48;
mining impact, 47; 1994 start,
44; subsidized food dumping, 45
Napo river, Ecuador, 1-3
National Institutes of Health (NIH),
73
NATO (North Atlantic Treaty
Organization), 34, 106
nature: capitalist 'worthlessness',
23; commodification, 93
Nazi Holocaust, 44; CPPCG
response to, 13
Negri, Antonio, 40
Neighbourhood Health Committees,
Venezuela, 127
New York Times, 99-100
NGOs (non-governmental
organizations), 103; hegemonic
role, 102; MDGs resources, 81
Nicaragua, 33, 130
Nixon, R., 35
non-food exports, for debt-
servicing, 66

Occidental oil, Ecuador drilling, 3
oil production, Venezuela, 147
'Operation Miracle', Cuba, 138
Organic Law of Hydrocarbons,
Venezuela, 122
Organs of People's Power (OPP),
Cuba, 132, 134
Oxfam, guiltless world-view, 9

Pakistan, 106
Panama, US invasion, 34
Paraguay, 129
participatory democracy, 113,
115-16, 124, 128, 134, 141, 153;
Cuba, 133, 147
peasants: seed saving knowledge,
57; 'question', 150
Pérez, Lisandro, 122-3
Pérez, Roberto, 145
pet food, Western spending, 82
Petrocaribe, 128
'petty bourgeoisie', global North, 105
Pfizer: Nigeria legal case

blackmailing, 72; Trovan drug
trials, 71
pharmaceuticals companies:
marketing spending, 71; R&D
decisions, 69-70; R&D price
rationalization, 79; structural
genocide, 68; testing practices,
73; US generic drugs lobbying,
76; US government support for,
80
philanthropy, capitalist, 8, 103-4
Pittis, Don, 35
Plan Colombia, 50
Poku, Nana K., 75
Pol Pot regime, Cambodia, 14, 19,
42, 141, 152
Polanyi, Karl, 22, 26
popular nationalism, global South,
33
Potash Corporation, Canada, 35
poverty, 1; rural Mexico, 46;
Venezuela reduction, 126
pregnancy and childbirth, African
deaths from, 64
preventable and treatable diseases,
44; deaths from, 7, 9, 11
primitive accumulation, 29-30, 85;
enclosure precondition, 31
privatization, 30, 37; global South,
104
property rights, prioritized, 27

Quichua indigenous group,
Ecuador, 2

Recife, Brazil, murders, 54
'red scares', 155
Refugee Convention, UN, 14
remittances, El Salvador
importance, 53
resource distribution, 11
rice, Mexican farmer NAFTA loss,
46
Roberts, David, 10, 96
Robinson, William I., 40
'rogue' nations, 107
Romero, Carlos, 145
'rule of law', 26-7
rural poverty, Mexico, 46
Russia, 118